BALAAM
THE SOOTHSAYER

The Prophet Who Would Not Listen

by Marilynn E. Hood

These books are available at special discounts when purchased in bulk for use as premiums, promotions, fundraising, or group studies. For inquiries and details, contact us: info@courageousheartpress.com.

Published by Courageous Heart Press
College Station, Texas

Editing and Interior Design by My Writers' Connection
Courageous Heart Press

Paperback ISBN: 978-1-950714-40-7
Library of Congress Control Number: 2024931760

To my grandfather, Ernest Lindsey Hasty (1894–1976), someone who loved God's Word and knew the value of searching the Scriptures.

"Beware of false prophets who come disguised as harmless sheep but are really vicious wolves. You can identify them by their fruit, that is, by the way they act."

—Matthew 7:15–16a, NLT

Contents

Author's Note

The idea for this book came to me as I studied the life of Moses for my book, *Moses: Called by God*. As I separated Moses's story from that of the Israelites, I read about Balaam, a Gentile soothsayer for hire. Tucked into the story of Balaam and his God-directed prophecies, Moses recorded a promise of the Messiah.

This discovery surprised me. Of course, I knew the story of "Balaam's Donkey." I'd heard it from my Sunday school teachers as a child and had read the passages many times as an adult. Perhaps I'd even seen the prophecy before, but as happens so often with God's Word, it struck me differently this time. My curiosity piqued, I made a few notes, and when I (finally) finished my study of Moses, I came back to Balaam.

My goal with this short book was to pull together the pieces of Balaam's story and discover what God might want us to learn from it.

The biblical account of Balaam can be divided into two parts:

- The oracles or prophecies Balaam spoke as instructed by God.
- The person of Balaam himself—his character.

A pagan king hired Balaam to curse the Israelites, but God commanded the soothsayer to speak only His truth regarding these people. Balaam's prophecies, therefore, told of God's relationship with the Israelites and provided a glimpse into their future and that of several other nations as well. They even told of the coming of the Messiah.

Acting on his own, however, Balaam deceitfully managed to facilitate one of the greatest episodes of sin that the Israelites engaged in during all their forty years of wandering.

The details of this dreadful incident lie scattered across several chapters of the book of Numbers, with a few bits of information found in the book of Joshua as well as in the New Testament. Why didn't Moses, as the scribe of the Pentateuch (the first five books of the Bible), compile all these pieces into one continuous account? Moses doesn't say. In fact, the humble leader of the Israelites rarely divulged anything of a personal nature in his writings. We can only speculate the reason for this scattered and drawn-out retelling, but we can do so in light of what we know about Moses:

- **He had been the one and only leader of the Israelites.** In the forty years prior to Balaam coming on the scene, Moses had led the Hebrews out of Egypt and organized them into the Israelite nation.

- **He had been responsible for teaching the Israelites about God's Law.** From the time God first delivered the Ten Commandments, Moses had been instructing the people in matters concerning the Law. He wanted to make sure they understood what God expected of them.

- **Moses had interceded for the people.** Time and again, the people had ignored God's sovereignty and His call for holiness. And time and again, Moses pleaded on their behalf for God's grace and mercy.

- **He had all but fulfilled his calling to lead the people to the Promised Land.** When the people fell as willing victims of Balaam's

deception, they were standing at the threshold of Canaan—the land God had promised to Abraham and his descendants centuries earlier.

- **Moses, however, knew he would not be allowed to enter this land.** At Meribah, he and Aaron sinned by taking credit for God's provision of water—they failed to give God the glory for the miracle He had empowered them to do. As a consequence, neither Moses nor Aaron was allowed to cross the Jordan River into the Promised Land.

- **Moses had pleaded with God to change His mind.** For the past forty years, Moses had striven to deliver the Israelites to the Promised Land. It's not surprising, then, that God's decree was difficult for Moses to accept. One of Moses's few personal requests recorded in Scripture was for God to change His mind and allow him to enter Canaan. Not only did God refuse, but He also instructed Moses not to speak to Him again concerning this matter. (See Deuteronomy 3:23-29.)

- **Moses had come to the end of his journey and the end of his life, and he knew it.** So, as Moses stated in Deuteronomy 3:29, there they stayed in the valley near Beth Peor. He knew that while the Israelites would later cross over into the Promised Land, he could go no farther.

It was then, while the Israelites were camped across the Jordan River from Canaan, that the leader of Moab, King Balak, summoned Balaam to curse God's people. God, however, had strictly warned Balaam that he could speak only what He instructed him to speak. As a result, Balaam was unable to curse the Israelites. But what Balaam did manage to do was to give King Balak an idea for how the people could be tempted to sin against their God. And sin they did.

With the Promised Land in sight, the Israelites forsook God's first commandment by worshipping Baal of Peor, the deity of the Moabites. Much like when they had worshipped the golden calf at Mount Sinai (Exodus 32), the people engaged in both idolatry and immoral behavior. God's punishment was swift and severe: 24,000 Israelites died on the plains of Moab—right across the river from Canaan.

We can only speculate as to why Moses didn't arrange all the pieces of this incident in a single passage, but my guess is that the memory was too painful to recount all at once. Imagine the grief and disappointment he must have felt as he witnessed the people sinning so openly against the God who had rescued, protected, and provided for them. Add to that the heartbreaking consequence of so many lives lost, coupled with the knowledge that all of this occurred during what he knew were his last days on earth. He may well have seen the Israelites' sin as a failure of all his years of leadership.

He may well have seen the Israelites' sin as a failure of all his years of leadership.

Although Moses could not enter the Promised Land with the children of Israel, God did allow him to look over and see it from afar. From atop Mount Nebo, God Himself gave Moses a bird's-eye tour of Canaan right before his death. Then, with his work on earth complete, God buried him there in Moab near Beth Peor. Moses fulfilled what God had called him to do; certainly, his rest would be well deserved.

Centuries later, Moses became one of the select few people ever to reappear on earth after his death. He, along with Elijah, stood with our Lord shortly before His crucifixion. The scriptures do not tell us which mountain served as the site of Jesus's transfiguration, but we can only suppose that Moses once again caught a glimpse of the Promised Land. This time, he stood with the promised Messiah—the same One whose foretelling he had captured in Balaam's prophecy. God honored Moses as only He could do in allowing him this encore appearance with our Savior. Clearly, the Almighty did not consider Moses's leadership a failure.

Since that time, no prophet has risen in Israel like Moses, whom the LORD knew face to face—no prophet who did all the signs and wonders that the LORD sent Moses to do in the land of Egypt to Pharaoh and to all his officials and all his land, and no prophet who performed all the mighty acts of power and awesome deeds that Moses did in the sight of all Israel.

—Deuteronomy 34:10–12, BSB

How to Use This Book

This study of Balaam can be done on its own or in conjunction with the study of Moses and the Israelites. The outline below lists the scripture readings that accompany each lesson, along with a suggested song to complete your devotionals.

Chapter	Chapter Title	Scripture Reading	Suggested Song	Song Links https://tinyurl.com/
Balaam Comes to Moab				
Setting the Scene	The Beginning of Balaam's Story			
Chapter 1	King Balak Sends for Balaam	Numbers 22:1–21	"Purer In Heart, O God"	zya4mpt4
Chapter 2	Balaam's Donkey Talks Back	Numbers 22:22–35	"Take My Life, and Let It Be"	mry8v6z6
Balaam's Oracles				
Chapter 3	Balaam's Oracles Begin	Numbers 22:36–23:12	"Is Thy Heart Right with God?"	yyyy2k5k
Chapter 4	Balaam's Second Oracle	Numbers 23:13–26	"Lord, Speak to Me"	27sz9uzv
Chapter 5	Oracle Number Three	Numbers 23:27–24:13	"Father, Hear the Prayer We Offer"	yh5vshk8
Chapter 6	The Fourth Oracle of Balaam	Numbers 24:14–19	"Star of the East"	4tcjr8d5
Chapter 7	The Final Three Oracles of Balaam	Numbers 24:20–25	"I Stand in Awe of You"	366e62t9
Israel Sins				
Chapter 8	The Seduction of Israel	Numbers 25	"Turn Your Eyes Upon Jesus"	23rhhvnc
Chapter 9	Taking Vengeance on the Midianites	Numbers 31:1–18, Joshua 13:15–23	"Nothing But the Blood"	36jchc65
Chapter 10	Wrapping It Up: The Second Census	Numbers 26	"To Canaan's Land I'm on My Way!"	2tj2cfnf

Use the "Thoughts to Ponder" questions at the end of each lesson to foster your personal study or to use for group discussions. I've shared my thoughts on these questions at the website, MarilynnHood.com/Balaam. Also at the website you can find an outline of the book as well as links to the suggested songs and resources cited.

May this study of Balaam be a meaningful one for you!

BALAAM COMES TO MOAB

Setting the Scene

The Beginning of Balaam's Story

If you recall anything about Balaam, it's probably that his donkey talked to him. While that's a memorable point, the prophecies entwined within his story are also noteworthy. As you search through the scriptures that accompany the chapters in this book, you'll discover the pieces to a sad and unfortunate event that occurred in the history of the Israelite people, even as they stood at the very threshold of the Promised Land. It carries with it a warning that has echoed down through the centuries and still speaks to us today. May we learn from this event and take its message to heart.

God's Promise

Centuries before Balaam was born, God made a promise to Abraham, Isaac, and Jacob (or Israel): Their descendants would inherit the land of Canaan. But God also told Abraham that, prior to receiving this inheritance, his descendants would endure years of slavery in Egypt.[1]

Everything happened as God had foretold. And when the children of Israel cried out for God's deliverance from their Egyptian slave masters, God called Moses to lead the people to freedom—and to a new life in the Promised Land.

It took an arduous forty-year journey through the wilderness, but as our story begins, God's

---

1

God called Abram in Genesis 12:1–4. God made a covenant with Abram in Genesis 15 and told him that a son from his own body would be his heir. In Genesis 15:13–21, God told him how his descendants would be enslaved in a country not their own and detailed the land they would inherit. In Genesis 17,

> Everything happened as God had foretold.

chosen people are finally about to witness the fulfillment of His promise to Abraham. Just across from their encampment near the Jordan River lay Jericho. Soon they would cross over and enter Canaan—the Promised Land.

Moab Perceives a Threat

During their time of wandering in the wilderness, God gave the Israelites specific instructions concerning certain people they would encounter along the way. Years earlier, He had awarded the Mount Seir region to Esau, the twin brother of Jacob. He warned the Israelites not to meddle with or harass Esau's descendants, the Edomites. God had also awarded land to the sons of Lot, the nephew of Abraham. His descendants were the Moabites and the Ammonites, and God told the Israelites He would not give them any of their land, either.[2]

During the final leg of their journey, the Israelites engaged in battle with the armies of two kings who were not part of these protected classes of people. Both kings held territories on the east side of the Jordan. In response to the Israelites' request to pass through his land, Sihon, the king of the Amorites, not only refused but came out against God's people with his entire army. Later, Og, the king of Bashan, led his army to attack the Israelites.[3] In both instances, and with God's help and protection, the Israelites defeated these armies and took possession of the land belonging to these kings. Moses later awarded their territories to the tribes of Reuben, Gad, and the half tribe of Manasseh.[4]

The Bible says that the people of Moab were "sick with dread because of the children of Israel" who had taken up camp on the plains of Moab across from Jericho (Numbers 22:3, NKJV). Perhaps King Balak didn't know God had instructed the Israelites to leave the Moabites alone. Maybe he felt pressured by his nation's citizens to do something to protect Moab. It's clear that

God established His covenant of circumcision and changed Abram's name to Abraham. In Genesis 26:1–6, God reaffirmed His promise to Isaac, Abraham's son. In Genesis 28:10–15, God reaffirmed His promise to Jacob, Isaac's son. In Genesis 35:9–13, God changed Jacob's name to Israel and again repeated His promise.

——————— 2 ———————

See Deuteronomy 2:1–8 for God's instructions concerning the land of the Edomites. In Deuteronomy 2:9–15, God tells the Israelites not to harass the Moabites, and in Deuteronomy 2:16–23, He repeats this warning concerning the Ammonites.

——————— 3 ———————

The account of the Israelites defeating Sihon, king of the Amorites, and Og, King of Bashan is given in Numbers 21:21–35.

——————— 4 ———————

Moses awarded the land east of the Jordan to these tribes on the condition that the men who were able to engage in battle cross over and help their fellow Israelites take possession of their land before returning to settle with their families. See Numbers 32 for this account, where it states in verse 33 that Moses gave them the land of Sihon and Og.

――――― 5 ―――――

See Numbers 21:25–31 for the account of the Amorites taking land from the former king of Moab. This land which the Israelites had just taken from the Amorites had once belonged to the Moabites.

The *Amorites* are not to be confused with the *Ammonites*. While the Ammonites were descendants of Lot through his son, Ben-Ammi, the Amorites were descendants of Canaan, a son of Ham, who was one of Noah's three sons. See Genesis 19:36–38 for an account of Lot's sons and Genesis 10:1, 6, 15–18 for the genealogy of the Amorites.

Balak knew the Amorites, who had defeated his predecessor and taken control of land that had once belonged to the Moabites, had now themselves been overtaken by the Israelites.[5]

Not wanting to lose face, more land, or be the next kingdom to fall, Balak took preemptive action against the Israelites. It is here that Balaam enters the story when Balak, the king of Moab, asks the Mesopotamian soothsayer to come to Moab and curse the Israelites.

The scriptures for the chapter readings come from the Berean Study Bible (BSB). You can download your own copy here: berean.bible/downloads.htm, or you can read it online by typing in a scripture at: biblehub.com. At that site, you can compare the BSB with other Bible versions by clicking on "Parallel" in the bar above the scripture or click "Comment" to read various commentaries on the scripture.

Thoughts to Ponder

King Balak made a decision without all the facts. How might this story have turned out differently had he known Moab had God's protection?

_____

_____

_____

_____

_____

When has fear led you to make an unwise decision? What was the outcome?

_____

_____

_____

_____

_____

What does the term *soothsayer* mean? Do you think it differs from being a prophet? If so, how?

_____

_____

_____

_____

_____

Chapter 1

King Balak Sends for Balaam

Numbers 22:1–21, BSB

(1) Then the Israelites traveled on and camped in the plains of Moab near the Jordan, across from Jericho.

(2) Now Balak son of Zippor saw all that Israel had done to the Amorites, (3) and Moab was terrified of the people because they were numerous. Indeed, Moab dreaded the Israelites. (4) So the Moabites said to the elders of Midian, "This horde will devour everything around us, as an ox licks up the grass of the field."

Since Balak son of Zippor was king of Moab at that time, (5) he sent messengers to Balaam son of Beor at Pethor, which is by the Euphrates in the land of his people.

"Behold, a people has come out of Egypt," said Balak. "They cover the face of the land and have settled next to me. (6) So please come now and put a curse on this people, because they are too mighty for me. Perhaps I may be able to defeat them and drive them out of the land; for I know that those you bless are blessed, and those you curse are cursed."

(7) The elders of Moab and Midian departed with the fees for divination in hand. They came to Balaam and relayed to him the words of Balak.

(8) "Spend the night here," Balaam replied, "and I will give you the answer that the LORD speaks to me." So the princes of Moab stayed with Balaam.

(9) Then God came to Balaam and asked, "Who are these men with you?"

(10) And Balaam said to God, "Balak son of Zippor, king of Moab, sent me this message (11) 'Behold, a people has come out of Egypt, and they cover the face of the land. Now come and put a curse on them for me. Perhaps I may be able to fight against them and drive them away.'"

(12) But God said to Balaam, "Do not go with them. You are not to curse this people, for they are blessed."

(13) So Balaam got up the next morning and said to Balak's princes, "Go back to your homeland, because the LORD has refused to let me go with you."

(14) And the princes of Moab arose, returned to Balak, and said, "Balaam refused to come with us."

(15) Then Balak sent other princes, more numerous and more distinguished than the first messengers.

(16) They came to Balaam and said, "This is what Balak son of Zippor says: 'Please let nothing hinder you from coming to me, (17) for I will honor you richly and do whatever you say. So please come and put a curse on this people for me!'"

(18) But Balaam replied to the servants of Balak, "If Balak were to give me his house full of silver and gold, I could not do anything small or great to go beyond the command of the LORD my God. (19) So now, please stay here overnight as the others did, that I may find out what else the LORD has to tell me."

(20) That night God came to Balaam and said, "Since these men have come to summon you, get up and go with them, but you must only do what I tell you." (21) So in the morning Balaam got up, saddled his donkey, and went with the princes of Moab.

◇◇◇

Suggested Song

"Purer In Heart, O God" (tinyurl.com/zya4mpt4)

———— 1 ————

Evidently, the Midianites lived among the Moabites at this point in time. Notice the references in verses 4 and 7 of this reading to the elders of Midian.

Fear-stricken, the Moabites watched this "horde" of Israelites make its way toward Canaan, coming to rest on the plains of Moab near the Jordan River.[1] The people complained to their local leaders, who brought their fears to Balak. The king likely knew the damage such an enormous group of people (not to mention their livestock) could do to the land of Moab. He also knew the Israelites had defeated the Amorites when King Sihon had refused them passage and tried to fight them. They had taken over Sihon's land and occupied his cities—land that had once belonged to Moab.

Now, these people were too close for comfort.

Having learned from others' mistakes, Balak opted not to engage the Israelites in battle—at least not until he had a tactical advantage. Instead, he took a different approach in hopes of gaining that advantage: He sent a request to a soothsayer named Balaam, who lived quite a distance away in Pethor in the Mesopotamian region by the Euphrates River.[2]

Balaam's reputation preceded him. Balak felt certain that if Balaam would curse the Israelites, he would then be able to defeat them—or at least drive them out of his country. And he was prepared to pay the hefty fee for Balaam's services.

When Balak's men arrived in Pethor and delivered his request, Balaam asked them to spend the night. He needed time to find out what God would say about this matter.

Indeed, God did come to Balaam and asked him who these men were. After Balaam explained to Him their mission, God instructed him not to go with them. Moreover, God told Balaam not to put a curse on the Israelites because they were a blessed people. When morning arrived, Balaam told Balak's princes to go home; God had refused to allow him to go with them.

King Balak remained undeterred by the report from his messengers. He responded by sending an even greater number of emissaries who were more distinguished than the first group. As before, they urged Balaam to come back with them. If only he would return with them and curse the Israelites, they told him, Balak would do whatever Balaam instructed and would reward him handsomely.

Once again, Balaam told this group of dignitaries to spend the night so he could find out if God had anything else to say. He warned them, however, that no matter how great a reward Balak might offer, he could do nothing more nor less than what God commanded him. As before, God came during the night to speak with Balaam. This time, however, He told Balaam to go with the men. But God cautioned him, "do only what I tell you" (Numbers 22:20, NIV).

———— 2 ————

In Joshua 13:22, Balaam is identified as someone who practiced divination. Various Bible versions state he was a soothsayer, an occult practitioner, someone who used magic to tell the future, an omen reader, or a fortune teller.

> If only he would return with them and curse the Israelites, they told him, Balak would do whatever Balaam instructed and would reward him handsomely.

What did Balaam's name mean?

According to commentators, Balaam's name meant "destruction of the people" or "the destroyer," and the name of his father, Beor, meant to "burn" or "consume." The meaning of their names has led Bible scholars to believe that Balaam likely belonged to a family whose profession was the dark arts or cursing.[3]

Much like participants in certain professions today give themselves a fearsome stage name (for example, wrestlers), it is thought the parents from divining families gave their children names according to their expectations— something for them to live up to. So, in today's world, Balaam might go by the nickname, "Balaam, the Destroyer."

———— 3 ————

Read more about what *Ellicott's Commentary for English Readers* and the *Pulpit Commentary* have to say concerning Balaam's name at "Commentaries: Numbers 22:5" (tinyurl.com/3vb8vwnc).

So Far, So Good

At this point in the story, Balaam has done only what God has told him to do. From his words and his actions, it appears he believes in God and respects His authority.

But what about the inclination of Balaam's heart?

It's important to remember that just because God uses someone for His purpose doesn't mean that person is righteous. And, unfortunately, just because someone believes in God doesn't always mean that person is a follower of God. As James 2:19 (NKJV) tells us, "You believe that there is one God. You do well. Even the demons believe—and tremble!" As for Balaam, time will soon reveal what he truly holds within his heart.

Do not stifle the Holy Spirit. Do not scoff at prophecies, but test everything that is said. Hold on to what is good. Stay away from every kind of evil.

—1 Thessalonians 5:19–22, NLT

Thoughts to Ponder

Did God really not know who the men were who came to Balaam in Numbers 22:9? Why do you think He asked Balaam this question?

_____

_____

_____

_____

_____

The second time Balak's emissaries approached Balaam, why did he not immediately send them away rather than again inquiring of God?

_____

_____

_____

_____

_____

What warning did God give the Israelites concerning divination and sorcery? See Leviticus 19:26b, 31. See also what Moses will soon tell them in Deuteronomy 18:9–14.

_____

_____

_____

_____

_____

Chapter 2

Balaam's Donkey Talks Back

Numbers 22:22–35, BSB

(22) Then God's anger was kindled because Balaam was going along, and the angel of the LORD stood in the road to oppose him. Balaam was riding his donkey, and his two servants were with him.

(23) When the donkey saw the angel of the LORD standing in the road with a drawn sword in his hand, she turned off the path and went into a field. So Balaam beat her to return her to the path.

(24) Then the angel of the LORD stood in a narrow passage between two vineyards, with walls on either side. (25) And the donkey saw the angel of the LORD and pressed herself against the wall, crushing Balaam's foot against it. So he beat her once again.

(26) And the angel of the LORD moved on ahead and stood in a narrow place where there was no room to turn to the right or left. (27) When the donkey saw the angel of the LORD, she lay down under Balaam, and he became furious and beat her with his staff.

(28) Then the LORD opened the donkey's mouth, and she said to Balaam, "What have I done to you that you have beaten me these three times?"

(29) Balaam answered the donkey, "You have made a fool of me! If I had a sword in my hand, I would kill you right now!"

(30) But the donkey said to Balaam, "Am I not the donkey you have ridden all your life until today? Have I ever treated you this way before?"

"No," he replied.

(31) Then the LORD opened Balaam's eyes, and he saw the angel of the LORD standing in the road with a drawn sword in his hand. And Balaam bowed low and fell facedown.

(32) The angel of the LORD asked him, "Why have you beaten your donkey these three times? Behold, I have come out to oppose you, because your way is perverse before me. (33) The donkey saw me and turned away

from me these three times. If she had not turned away, then by now I would surely have killed you and let her live."

(34) "I have sinned," Balaam said to the angel of the LORD, "for I did not realize that you were standing in the road to confront me. And now, if this is displeasing in your sight, I will go back home."

(35) But the angel of the LORD said to Balaam, "Go with the men, but you are to speak only what I tell you." So Balaam went with the princes of Balak.

◇◇◇

Suggested Song

"Take My Life, and Let It Be" (tinyurl.com/mry8v6z6)

If you've ever been around donkeys, you probably know they tend to balk when they decide they don't want to obey their handler's commands. Particularly when startled or frightened, they may simply stop and refuse to budge, go their own direction, or even lay down. Unlike horses who tend to run when frightened, donkeys often turn their heads and try to ignore what's scaring them. Because they are quite strong for their size, tugging on their lead rope or reins usually doesn't work—at all. The handler must figure out what's bothering the donkey first and either remedy the problem to the donkey's satisfaction or outsmart him.

But even if you've never been around donkeys at all, you can probably guess that beating an animal is often counterproductive. In our day and age, most people wouldn't be expected to know much about handling donkeys. However, in many parts of the world, from Bible times all the way up to the early 1900's when automobiles began to take over, almost everyone did know at least something about donkeys and their behavior.[1]

You can be certain the people who were accompanying Balaam as they headed out to Moab knew about handling donkeys. Don't you wonder what was going through their minds when they saw this famous soothsayer repeatedly beating his own donkey? Obviously here was a man not in control—either of his donkey or of himself.

1

If you're interested in donkeys, this site provides a wealth of practical information: The Donkey Listener (tinyurl.com/2r58an7s).

This article from BBC.com discusses the important roles donkeys have played for centuries: "How Donkeys Changed the Course of Human History" (tinyurl.com/5bjdwj2n).

Off to a Shaky Start

The donkey saw, or at least sensed, what Balaam could not. An angel of the Lord stood in Balaam's path, ready to kill him if necessary. (It's gratifying to know the angel would have spared the donkey.) The creature's actions—or rather inaction—may well have saved Balaam's life. But why did the angel of the Lord block Balaam's path after God had given him permission to go to Balak?

God is faithful in word and deed and does not behave arbitrarily. In fact, Balaam will soon act as God's own mouthpiece and utter these words in his second oracle: "God is not human, that he should lie, not a human being, that he should change his mind. Does he speak and then not act? Does he promise and not fulfill?" (Numbers 23:19, NIV).

No, God is not fickle, but He does possess omniscient foresight. As He read the thoughts that were forming in Balaam's mind, He knew Balaam wasn't heading to see King Balak out of the goodness of his heart or because he believed in Balak's cause and wanted to right a wrong. God saw that Balaam's concern was with enriching himself, both in wealth and in prestige, and he was trying to figure out how to attain both without specifically disobeying God. While the intent of Balaam's heart won't be revealed to us until later, the angel, by declaring that his way was "perverse" before the Lord, tells us that God already knew Balaam's heart had turned down the wrong path.

Until this point in the story, the Bible hasn't revealed much about Balaam as a person. We know that he sought God's permission before embarking on the long journey back to Moab and that he is insistent he can only say what God permits him to say. If it weren't for his reputation for being proficient at cursing people, you might think he was a pretty decent guy—until he starts beating his donkey.

> If it weren't for his reputation for being proficient at cursing people, you might think he was a pretty decent guy—until he starts beating his donkey.

With his repeated angry outbursts, Balaam reveals quite a bit about his character. He admitted that his donkey had served him faithfully for many years, but when she refused to go where he wanted her to, he didn't bother to figure out why. He simply beat her until she relented to his control. Why? He was embarrassed.

Balaam's concern was that the animal had made him look like a fool in front of the king's emissaries and his own servants. It was a valid concern. He had been summoned to curse a nation, which presumably meant he possessed the power to influence future events or control people or circumstances. Since God had to open Balaam's eyes in order for him to see the angel of the Lord, it's likely that no one else heard the donkey talking or saw the angel blocking Balaam's way. The others would only have seen him beating and screaming at what appeared to be an unruly donkey.

Balaam may have feared that those watching the scene would tell the king that he was an imbecile incapable of controlling his own donkey. But as much as he hated to look like a fool, it would have been worse if word got back to the king that he was a fraud.

Greed was Balaam's incentive.

Pride was his concern.

Anger and violence were his response to a situation (and to a donkey) he couldn't control.

Anytime you're worried about appearing to be a fool, stop and think about Balaam and question your motives. Are your actions and concerns motivated by a pure heart, or have you acted deceitfully? If the intent of your heart is to do what is right, then it doesn't matter what others may think. On the other hand, if you cringe at the thought of God searching your heart and discovering your true motive, then it's time to turn your donkey around and head in a different direction.

"As for you, Solomon my son, know the God of your father, and serve Him with a whole heart and a willing mind, for the LORD searches every heart and understands the intention of every thought. If you seek Him, He will be found by you, but if you forsake Him, He will reject you forever."

—1 Chronicles 28:9, HCSB

Thoughts to Ponder

When Balaam finally saw the angel before him, he asked for forgiveness and offered to turn around and go home. What did the angel tell Balaam? What point was God trying to make certain Balaam truly understood when He sent His angel to stop Balaam? Why do you think God found it necessary to reiterate His instructions in such a dramatic fashion?

_____

_____

_____

_____

More than speaking words to Balaam, his donkey actually reasoned with him. Why didn't Balaam find it astounding that his donkey was speaking to him? Why was he unable to immediately recognize God's divine intervention in this situation? Have there been occurrences in your life where you were so focused on yourself and your needs that you failed to see the bigger picture?

_____

_____

_____

_____

Can you think of other examples of someone whose eyes were opened to see the spiritual world? A dramatic example is given in 2 Kings 6:8–23. Note particularly the happenings in verses 16–17.

_____

_____

_____

_____

BALAAM'S ORACLES

Chapter 3

Balaam's Oracles Begin

Numbers 22:36–23:12, BSB

(22:36) When Balak heard that Balaam was coming, he went out to meet him at the Moabite city on the Arnon border, at the edge of his territory. (37) And he said to Balaam, "Did I not send you an urgent summons? Why did you not come to me? Am I really not able to richly reward you?"

(38) "See, I have come to you," Balaam replied, "but can I say just anything? I must speak only the word that God puts in my mouth."

(39) So Balaam accompanied Balak, and they came to Kiriath-huzoth. (40) Balak sacrificed cattle and sheep, and he gave portions to Balaam and the princes who were with him.

(41) The next morning, Balak took Balaam and brought him up to Bamoth-baal. From there he could see the outskirts of the camp of the people.

(23:1) Then Balaam said to Balak, "Build for me seven altars here, and prepare for me seven bulls and seven rams."

(2) So Balak did as Balaam had instructed, and Balak and Balaam offered a bull and a ram on each altar.

(3) "Stay here by your burnt offering while I am gone," Balaam said to Balak. "Perhaps the LORD will meet with me. And whatever He reveals to me, I will tell you."

So Balaam went off to a barren height, (4) and God met with him. "I have set up seven altars," Balaam said, "and on each altar I have offered a bull and a ram."

(5) Then the LORD put a message in Balaam's mouth, saying, "Return to Balak and give him this message."

(6) So he returned to Balak, who was standing there beside his burnt offering, with all the princes of Moab.

(7) And Balaam lifted up an oracle, saying:

"Balak brought me from Aram,

the king of Moab from the mountains of the east.

'Come,' he said, 'put a curse on Jacob for me; come and denounce Israel!'

(8) How can I curse what God has not cursed?

How can I denounce what the LORD has not denounced?

(9) For I see them from atop the rocky cliffs, and I watch them from the hills.

Behold, a people dwelling apart, not reckoning themselves among the nations.

(10) Who can count the dust of Jacob or number even a fourth of Israel?

Let me die the death of the righteous; let my end be like theirs!"

(11) Then Balak said to Balaam, "What have you done to me? I brought you here to curse my enemies, and behold, you have only blessed them!"

(12) But Balaam replied, "Should I not speak exactly what the LORD puts in my mouth?"

◇◇◇

Suggested Song

"Is Thy Heart Right with God?"
(tinyurl.com/yyyy2k5k)

———— 1 ————

King Balak seems to have wasted no time in sending his emissaries for Balaam. News travels fast, and he already knew all that Israel had done to the Amorites (Numbers 22:2). While it would have taken time for his people to reach Balaam's home, they were probably able to travel fairly quickly over established routes. Unlike the Israelites who traveled more slowly, they did not have children or livestock to

How long did King Balak have to wait for his emissaries to return with Balaam? We are not told, but the distance they had to travel from Moab to where Balaam lived in Mesopotamia had to have been several hundred miles. With an average day's journey in Bible times being about 25–30 miles, a round trip may have taken several weeks.[1]

You can imagine Balak pacing the floors as he waited for word, wondering if Balaam would come this time or not. He had waited for his first emissaries to return, only to learn that Balaam had declined his request. It was possible the soothsayer would refuse to come this time as well.

When Balak finally received word Balaam was on the way, he couldn't wait any longer. The king traveled to the edge of his territory to meet him and escort him back.

You can hear the frustration and impatience in Balak's voice as he chided Balaam for not coming sooner. But Balaam came right back at him, his response laced with arrogance and an equal amount of impatience. He then proceeded to inform Balak he could speak only the words God put in his mouth. If the king had known then what those words were going to be, he would have sent Balaam right back home!

Balak escorted Balaam and his emissaries on into Moab and made sacrifices of oxen and sheep so he could feed them. He wanted them to be ready in the morning to begin the cursing.

At some point during this whole account, you may have wondered why Balak had placed so much hope in Balaam, a foreigner he evidently knew only by his reputation. Why had he not sought the assistance of his god, Baal? We can only surmise that Balak saw what had happened to the other kings whom the Israelites had defeated and realized that their false gods had failed miserably to protect them. He was desperate for some other way to defend his country.

The next morning, Balak took Balaam up to a vantage point where they could view a portion of the Israelite people.[2] From there, Balaam spoke his first oracle, a proclamation from God concerning His people. In it, God reminded them both who His people were: A holy people, literally set apart by God for His purposes. "Behold, a people dwelling apart, not reckoning themselves among the nations."[3] Could this line have given Balaam his deceitful and deadly idea as to how to obey God's directive and still collect his reward from Balak?

His Words Sounded Right

With his words, Balaam seemed to indicate a desire to live a righteous life. His later actions, however, proved that his heart was not in those words. Even though God had used him as His mouthpiece, Balaam did not serve God. The words that passed through his lips failed to pierce his heart. And because of his hard heart toward God, Balaam would not die the death of the righteous, as he had said he desired.

> The words that passed through his lips failed to pierce his heart.

——— 2 ———

care for along the way and could travel longer hours at a time.

The Israelite's massive numbers and the substantial needs of their livestock likely meant that their encampment stretched for several miles. Only a portion of them could be seen from any one place. This particular high place was named for Baal and was quite likely one of the places where the pagan god was worshipped. This article provides more information on high places: "What is the significance of high places in the Bible?" (tinyurl.com/pj7x6hnx). This article provides quite a bit of information concerning Baal: "The Worship of Baal" (tinyurl.com/y885b2xe).

——— 3 ———

See Numbers 23:9b, BSB.

——— 4 ———

Balak and Balaam were both so determined to accomplish their own goals that they hardened their hearts and refused to listen to what God was telling them. The writer of Hebrews admonishes us not to let sin's deceitfulness harden our hearts: "See to it, brothers, that none of you has a wicked heart of unbelief that turns away from the living God. But exhort one another daily, as long as it is called today, so that none of you may be hardened by sin's deceitfulness" (Hebrews 3:12–13, BSB).

If Balaam had been wise, he would have paid heed to the words that God had spoken through him. He would have sought to align his heart with God's Word.

It's the same for us today. We hear His Word when we read and study the scriptures. Then it's up to us to incline our hearts toward God, to listen to what He's telling us and then respond to His Word with faith and sincerity.[4]

Our words, our thoughts, and our actions all need to be in alignment with our hearts, and our hearts need to be turned toward God. As David prayed so long ago, "Let the words of my mouth and the meditation of my heart be acceptable in your sight, O LORD, my rock and my redeemer" (Psalm 19:14, ESV).

"These people honor me with their lips, but their hearts are far from me."

—Matthew 15:8, NIV

Balaam was from Pethor, which was situated in Mesopotamia on the Euphrates River. It was not far from the city of Haran.

You may recall that Abraham also came from Mesopotamia. He first lived in Ur of the Chaldeans and then traveled to Haran where he and his family lived for a period of time. Upon the death of his father, Terah, Abraham and his family then came on to Canaan, as God had called him to do.

Abraham had a brother, Nahor, who also came at some point to live in Haran in Mesopotamia. Evidently, he and his family continued to live there for quite some time. When Abraham's son Isaac came of age to marry, Abraham did not want him to take a wife from among the Canaanites. He sent his servant to Mesopotamia to where Nahor lived to find a wife for Isaac from among his kinsmen (Genesis 24:10). Later, Isaac sent his son Jacob to Mesopotamia to Padan Aram (evidently the same place as Haran) for him to find a wife from among their kinsmen as well (Genesis 28:5, 10).

Although Abraham left Mesopotamia several centuries earlier than when Balaam lived there, it's likely he still had relatives living near the area where Balaam lived. It's also likely that the news of the Israelites' escape from Egypt and the destruction of Pharaoh and his army had spread far and wide during the forty years the Israelites were wandering in the wilderness.

So, when King Balak sent for Balaam to curse a people who had come from Egypt and were so numerous that they covered the face of the earth (Numbers 22:5–6), Balaam probably knew exactly who he was being asked to curse. Certainly, he was acquainted with their God who told him they were a blessed people (Numbers 22:12). As Balaam stated several times in his oracles (Numbers 24:4, 16), his eyes truly were wide open. He knew what he was doing, but he overestimated his own abilities and underestimated the God of the Israelites.

Thoughts to Ponder

How many altars did God's people usually erect in any one place? What did the plurality of altars that Balaam built seem to indicate? What did the number seven symbolize to the Hebrews? This article provides more information: "What Does the Number 7 Mean in the Bible and Why is it Important?" (tinyurl.com/yck26met).

_____

_____

_____

_____

In Numbers 23:9b (NIV), Balaam observed the Israelites to be "a people who live apart and do not consider themselves one of the nations." What commands did God give the Israelites concerning their relationships with other nations, particularly those who currently occupied Canaan? What reasons did God give for His commands? (See Deuteronomy 7:1-6.)

_____

_____

_____

_____

What does the "dust of Jacob" refer to in Numbers 23:10?

_____

_____

_____

_____

Chapter 4

Balaam's Second Oracle

Numbers 23:13–26, BSB

(13) Then Balak said to him, "Please come with me to another place where you can see them. You will only see the outskirts of their camp—not all of them. And from there, curse them for me."

(14) So Balak took him to the field of Zophim, to the top of Pisgah, where he built seven altars and offered a bull and a ram on each altar.

(15) Balaam said to Balak, "Stay here beside your burnt offering while I meet the LORD over there."

(16) And the LORD met with Balaam and put a message in his mouth, saying, "Return to Balak and speak what I tell you."

(17) So he returned to Balak, who was standing there by his burnt offering with the princes of Moab.

"What did the LORD say?" Balak asked.

(18) Then Balaam lifted up an oracle, saying:

"Arise, O Balak, and listen; give ear to me, O son of Zippor.

(19) God is not a man, that He should lie, or a son of man, that He should change His mind.

Does He speak and not act?

Does He promise and not fulfill?

(20) I have indeed received a command to bless; He has blessed, and I cannot change it.

(21) He considers no disaster for Jacob; He sees no trouble for Israel.

The LORD their God is with them, and the shout of the King is among them.

(22) God brought them out of Egypt with strength like a wild ox.

(23) For there is no spell against Jacob and no divination against Israel.

It will now be said of Jacob and Israel, 'What great things God has done!'

(24) Behold, the people rise like a lioness; they rouse themselves like a lion, not resting until they devour their prey and drink the blood of the slain."

(25) Now Balak said to Balaam, "Then neither curse them at all nor bless them at all!"

(26) But Balaam replied, "Did I not tell you that whatever the LORD says, I must do?"

Suggested Song

"Lord, Speak to Me" (tinyurl.com/27sz9uzv)

——— 1 ———

See Numbers 23:24, BSB.

Did you sense a difference in this second oracle as compared to the first? For one thing, it's longer. For another, there is a shift in the tone. God issued a rather polite warning in the first one, but in this one, you can tell He's getting serious.

After admonishing Balak to listen up and pay attention to what he had to say, God revealed one of His prime attributes—He does what He says He will do! God then proceeded to explain His love for and devotion to the descendants of Jacob: The Israelites are a blessed people against whom omens and divinations will not work. In fact, others will see them and declare, *Look what great things God has done for Israel!*

> God revealed one of His prime attributes—He does what He says He will do!

God ended His second message to Balak with a warning: The strength and courage of the Israelites in attacking their enemies will be like that of a lioness. They will not stop in their pursuit until they have slain them; they will not rest until they *"devour their prey and drink the blood of the slain."*[1]

Failing to Listen to God

What a powerful warning God issued to Balak (and to Balaam) in this oracle! His message was clear:

- The Israelites served a powerful God.

- All efforts to curse them would be futile.

- To become their enemy would prove deadly.

Both Balak and Balaam heard God's words, but neither had the wisdom to heed His message. Balak simply refused to listen. He was so intent upon seeing the Israelites cursed that he continued in his efforts, even after hearing God's warning.

Balaam, blinded by his greed, lacked the good sense to give up and go home. God warned him repeatedly not to go against Him before he arrived in Moab, and now He had warned him twice through His oracles. Yet rather than yield to God's authority, Balaam persisted in trying to please Balak in order to gain prestige and a monetary reward.

Do you sometimes hear God's Word but fail to listen to what He's telling you? When you study your Bible, take a moment to pray for your heart to be receptive to His Word. Pray for the wisdom to understand the scriptures and the courage to apply them. As the life of Balaam illustrates so well, hearing the Word is not enough. We must also listen with our hearts.

Your word is a lamp to my feet and a light to my path.

—Psalm 119:105, NKJV

Moses wrote the book of Deuteronomy while the Israelites were camped on the plains of Moab across from Jericho. During this same time, Balaam uttered his oracles as he looked down upon the people from various high places. By combining several scriptures, we learn it took Moses about one month to write Deuteronomy during the last days of his life:

- He started his discourse on the first day of the eleventh month in the fortieth year after they left Egypt (Deuteronomy 1:3–5).

- After his death in Deuteronomy 34, the Israelites mourned for Moses for thirty days while they were still camped on the plains of Moab (Deuteronomy 34:8).

- The Israelites celebrated their first Passover in Canaan on the plains of Jericho at twilight on the fourteenth day of the first month of the next year (Joshua 5:10).

Working backwards from that first Passover in Canaan, we can deduce that Moses had about a month to write Deuteronomy (during the eleventh month), and then the Israelites had thirty days to mourn Moses after his death (during the twelfth month). The roughly two weeks of the first month of the new year were spent spying out Jericho which took at least three days (Joshua 2:1, 22), camping down by the river for three days (Joshua 3:1–5), crossing the Jordan River on the tenth day of the first month (Joshua 4:19), circumcising all the uncircumcised males (Joshua 5:2–7), and then staying in camp until they had healed (Joshua 5:8). Recall that the males needed to be circumcised before they could partake of the Passover.

So finally, in the forty-first year after leaving Egypt, the Israelites were able to celebrate Passover in the land of Canaan which God had promised to Abraham so long ago. They ate the produce of the land on the day after Passover (Joshua 5:11), and then the following day, the manna ceased (Joshua 5:12). From then on, they ate the food of the land of Canaan, a land flowing with milk and honey.

Thoughts to Ponder

In the New King James Version of the Bible, the passage in Numbers 23:21 reads like this: "He has not observed iniquity in Jacob, Nor has He seen wickedness in Israel. The LORD his God is with him, And the shout of a King is among them." (Compare various other versions of Numbers 23:21 at BibleHub.com: tinyurl.com/bp79kr4m. Also at this site, you can read commentaries on this scripture at tinyurl.com/5xekyjrn.)

What sins had Israel committed since their deliverance from Egypt? Why did they have to wander in the wilderness for forty years before they could enter the Promised Land?

In view of all the sins the Israelites had committed, what does this verse reveal about the character of God?

_____

_____

_____

Again referring to Numbers 23:21, what does this mean: "The LORD his God is with him, And the shout of a King is among them"?

_____

_____

_____

In Numbers 23:24, the Israelites are likened to a lion and lioness. How does this comparison hold special meaning for God's people? (See Genesis 49:9–12, Isaiah 31:4, and Revelation 5:5.)

These articles discuss the meaning of the "Lion of Judah":

- "Who/what is the Lion of the tribe of Judah?" (tinyurl.com/2p92wj5n)
- "4 Powerful Reasons to Understand and Know Jesus as the Lion of Judah" (tinyurl.com/4224env4)

_____

_____

_____

Chapter 5

Oracle Number Three

Numbers 23:27–24:13, BSB

(23:27) "Please come," said Balak, "I will take you to another place. Perhaps it will please God that you curse them for me from there."

(28) And Balak took Balaam to the top of Peor, which overlooks the wasteland.

(29) Then Balaam said, "Build for me seven altars here, and prepare for me seven bulls and seven rams."

(30) So Balak did as Balaam had instructed, and he offered a bull and a ram on each altar.

(24:1) And when Balaam saw that it pleased the LORD to bless Israel, he did not resort to sorcery as on previous occasions, but he turned his face toward the wilderness. (2) When Balaam looked up and saw Israel encamped tribe by tribe, the Spirit of God came upon him, (3) and he lifted up an oracle, saying:

"This is the prophecy of Balaam son of Beor, the prophecy of a man whose eyes are open,

(4) the prophecy of one who hears the words of God, who sees a vision from the Almighty, who bows down with eyes wide open:

(5) How lovely are your tents, O Jacob, your dwellings, O Israel!

(6) They spread out like palm groves, like gardens beside a stream,

like aloes the LORD has planted, like cedars beside the waters.

(7) Water will flow from his buckets, and his seed will have abundant water.

His king will be greater than Agag, and his kingdom will be exalted.

(8) God brought him out of Egypt with strength like a wild ox, to devour hostile nations and crush their bones, to pierce them with arrows.

(9) He crouches, he lies down like a lion; like a lioness, who dares to rouse him? Blessed

are those who bless you and cursed are those who curse you."

(10) Then Balak's anger burned against Balaam, and he struck his hands together and said to Balaam, "I summoned you to curse my enemies, but behold, you have persisted in blessing them these three times. (11) Therefore, flee at once to your home! I said I would richly reward you, but instead the LORD has denied your reward."

(12) Balaam answered Balak, "Did I not already tell the messengers you sent me (13) that even if Balak were to give me his house full of silver and gold, I could not do anything of my own accord, good or bad, to go beyond the command of the LORD? I will speak whatever the LORD says."

Suggested Song

"Father, Hear the Prayer We Offer"
(tinyurl.com/yh5vshk8)

You can feel the level of Balak's frustration increase with each oracle. After the second one, he told Balaam to just stop and not do anything. If he couldn't curse the Israelites, saying nothing would be better than heaping even more blessings upon them.

But Balak didn't really mean what he said. Instead, he moved Balaam over to another vantage point so he could try again. Baal worship was common in many of the high places, so maybe he thought he could find a spot where Baal's spirit might help them out. Or perhaps he was trying to find a place that offered a better view of this massive group of people. No matter what motivated him to keep moving, Balak stubbornly refused to give up.

With the first two oracles, Balaam stepped away from the altars to meet with God. This time, he didn't do that. Instead, when he looked out upon the Israelites camped by their tribes, the Spirit of God came upon him. And then, Balaam delivered yet another prophecy proclaiming prosperity and greatness for the Israelites.

By now, Balak's anger had reached the boiling point. He had summoned Balaam to curse his enemies, but he had only blessed them instead—and warned everyone else not to oppose them. It seemed Balak, rather than the Israelites, was worse off than before. Certainly, he was out the twenty-one bulls and twenty-one rams that had been sacrificed, as well as all the time and effort it had taken him to summon Balaam, climb up and down all those mountains, and build the twenty-one altars.

This time, Balak was through with Balaam. He clapped his hands together and told him to go home. And even though he had promised to reward him for his services, Balak now refused to do so. "I said I would reward you handsomely," he told Balaam, "but the LORD has kept you from being rewarded" (Numbers 24:11, NIV). Balaam had failed to curse the Israelites. It now appeared he would be forced to leave empty-handed.

Third Time—Still No Charm!

Regardless of whether Balaam had ever been a faithful follower of the Lord or not, he plainly acknowledged in the third oracle that he heard His words loud and clear as God spoke through him. Why, then, would Balaam be complicit in trying repeatedly to curse people whom God had clearly blessed? Why didn't he remove himself from the whole situation, particularly after the Spirit of God had willingly come upon him in the third oracle?

Balaam was not ignorant. He knew who God was and willfully chose to sin against Him. Did he not understand the repercussions of the words he spoke? God's message was clear: "Blessed are those who bless you and cursed are those who curse you" (Numbers 24:9, BSB). Seeking their own gain, the prophet and king stubbornly refused to heed God's warning—which Balaam had uttered with his own lips—and now they were doomed.

God could have ended these attempts to curse the Israelites in an instant—if He had desired. Instead, He gave Balaam multiple opportunities to

> Seeking their own gain, the prophet and king stubbornly refused to heed God's warning, and now they were doomed.

Moses is credited with writing the first five books of our Bible: Genesis, Exodus, Leviticus, Numbers, and Deuteronomy. They are collectively referred to as the Pentateuch. However, Moses did not assign any of these names to his writings. He evidently wrote everything on one scroll and simply referred to it as the "book" or "book of the law." Centuries later, it is surmised that Greek translators divided Moses's writings into the five parts we have in our Bibles today and gave them their titles.[1]

Shortly before his death in Moab, when Moses had finished writing in the book, he handed it over to the Levites who carried the Ark of the Covenant. He instructed them to place it beside the ark. At the end of every seven years, in the year for canceling debts during the Feast of Tabernacles, he told them they were to read God's Law before the people. They were to assemble everyone— men, women, children, and the aliens who lived in their towns—so they could all listen to God's Word. In so doing, the people would learn to both fear the Lord and carefully follow the words of the Law. The repeated reading of God's Word through the years would also serve as a way for them to pass down the Law to their children. (See Deuteronomy 31:9–13, 24–26.)

——— 1 ———

For more information, see "Pentateuch, The" in *Smith's Bible Dictionary* (tinyurl.com/5xcv6zv7). Also see "Deuteronomy" in *Easton's Bible Dictionary* (tinyurl.com/48cn25vh).

recognize His authority and change his ways. But Balaam chose not to do so. He never turned his heart toward God.

Can you think of a time when God gave you the opportunity to do the right thing, but you chose your own way instead? Perhaps you doggedly continued in your error, or maybe you shrank away and failed to take a stand or speak up for what was right. Be persistent in studying God's Word so that you will know the right thing to say or do when opportunities arise. There will come a time, as it did for Balaam, when you will be afforded no more opportunities to turn to Him and do what is right.

"The grass withers, the flower fades, But the word of our God stands forever."

—Isaiah 40:8, NKJV

Thoughts to Ponder

How do we know that Balaam understood the words he was prophesying? (See Numbers 24:3–4.)

_____

_____

_____

_____

In Numbers 24:2, the scriptures state that Balaam looked out and saw Israel camped according to their tribes. Then he described the tents of Jacob in verses 5–6. How were the Israelites to arrange their camp? What should the orderly arrangement of such an enormous group of people and animals have indicated to both Balaam and Balak? What would you think if you had looked down upon their encampment? See Numbers 2, where God gave a detailed description for the layout of the Israelite camp. This article presents a description and drawing of how their camp was to be set up: "Encampment of the Tribes of Israel in the Wilderness" (tinyurl.com/jf893s23).

_____

_____

_____

_____

While describing the Israelites in Numbers 24:8–9, how did God again give a warning to Balak and Balaam?

_____

_____

_____

_____

Chapter 6

The Fourth Oracle of Balaam

Numbers 24:14–19, BSB

(14) Now I am going back to my people, but come, let me warn you what this people will do to your people in the days to come."

(15) Then Balaam lifted up an oracle, saying,

"This is the prophecy of Balaam son of Beor, the prophecy of a man whose eyes are open,

(16) the prophecy of one who hears the words of God, who has knowledge from the Most High,

who sees a vision from the Almighty, who bows down with eyes wide open:

(17) I see him, but not now; I behold him, but not near.

A star will come forth from Jacob, and a scepter will arise from Israel.

He will crush the skulls of Moab and strike down all the sons of Sheth.

(18) Edom will become a possession, as will Seir, his enemy; but Israel will perform with valor.

(19) A ruler will come from Jacob and destroy the survivors of the city."

King Balak may have been through with Balaam, but God was not. He had much more to say through this soothsayer who served as His mouthpiece. His fourth oracle would hold profound implications concerning the future of the Israelites, their enemies, and ultimately the world.

In this oracle, Balaam described a future ruler who would rise out of Israel. He would be exceptional, a "star." He would also

Suggested Song

"Star of the East" (tinyurl.com/4tcjr8d5)

Along with Moab, the prophecy mentions the "sons of Sheth" in verse 17 of this reading. Other versions may instead mention Seth or translate this term as "sons of tumult." If "Seth" is the true rendering, then Seth, as the son of Adam, would evidently stand for all mankind, as any other descendants of Adam would have been destroyed in the flood. We can only surmise that either of these terms referred to people who caused trouble for the Israelites.

See Deuteronomy 2:2–6 for God's instructions concerning the descendants of Esau. His instructions concerning the Moabites are in Deuteronomy 2:9 and those concerning the Ammonites in Deuteronomy 2:17–19.

Note: The *Ammonites* are not to be confused with the *Amorites*. While the Ammonites were descendants of Lot, the Amorites were descendants of Canaan, a son of Ham, who was

possess the authority of a king, as indicated by his "scepter," the ornamental staff carried by rulers, and he would subdue both Moab and Edom.[1]

At this point, a brief review of the history of these nations is in order. Recall that the Moabites and the Edomites were relatives of the Israelites. Moab and his brother Ben-Ammi (whose descendants were the Ammonites) were the sons of Lot, the nephew of Abraham. The Edomites were even more closely related. They were the descendants of Esau, the brother of Jacob (whose name God later changed to Israel).

During the forty-year journey of the Israelites to the Promised Land, God had protected the land of the Moabites, Edomites, and Ammonites. Concerning the Edomites, God had given these instructions to the Israelites: "Do not provoke them to war, for I will not give you any of their land, not even enough to put your foot on. I have given Esau the hill country of Seir as his own" (Deuteronomy 2:5, NIV). Moreover, the Israelites were to pay them in silver for any food or water they consumed while passing through.

Concerning the Moabites and Ammonites, God also instructed the Israelites not to harass them as they journeyed. However, His warnings concerning these nations were not as extensive as the one He had issued for the Edomites.[2]

What caused God in this oracle to lift His divine protection from the land of the Moabites and Edomites? For one thing, the Moabites had failed to show hospitality toward their kinsmen, the Israelites, and even went so far as to hire Balaam to curse them. But it's what they will do in the very next chapter, Numbers 25, that truly sets God's anger against them. Their despicable behavior will play a major role in causing the Israelites to sin grievously.

As for the Edomites, the struggle between Jacob and Esau began in the womb. Before the birth of her twins, God told their mother, Rebekah, that the older son, Esau, would serve the younger son, Jacob.[3]

Jacob took both Esau's birthright and his inheritance. This sparked an unrest that eventually subsided a bit during their lifetimes but later framed the tenuous relationship that existed between their descendants. The Israelites and the Edomites had been at odds for generations, and further in Scripture, we see that the animosity continued to burn. The Edomites, whom God had previously protected, ended up engaging in numerous hostilities and atrocities against the Israelites. King David finally conquered them, but the enmity between these nations remained.

The "Star" and the "Scepter"

Although this oracle doesn't indicate who the future ruler would be, we do know from an earlier prophecy that Judah was slated to be a leader among his brothers. It was Israel who foretold this when he bestowed his blessings upon his sons shortly before his death. "Judah," he told him in Genesis 49:8 (NIV), "your brothers will praise you; your hand will be on the neck of your enemies; your father's sons will bow down to you." Israel continued his blessing by telling of the rulers who would come from Judah. He stated, "The scepter will not depart from Judah, nor the ruler's staff from between his feet, until he to whom it belongs shall come and the obedience of the nations shall be his" (Genesis 49:10, NIV).

History bears out that the prophecies foretold in this fourth oracle were at least partly fulfilled during the time of King David, who was from the tribe of Judah. Known as a man after God's own heart,[4] he conquered many nations in developing the land of Canaan for Israel, including Moab and Edom. Yet, while these two nations were subdued during his reign, they continued to cause problems for Israel through the centuries.

one of Noah's three sons (Genesis 10:6, 15–18). The Amorites were not under God's protection.

———— 3 ————

See Genesis 25:21–23.

———— 4 ————

When King Saul failed to keep God's command, God took the kingship from him and gave it to David. The prophet Samuel told Saul that his kingdom would not endure, and that God had sought out a man after His own heart. See 1 Samuel 13:13–14.

———— 5 ————

The Apostle Paul explains in Colossians 2:15 that Christ disarmed principalities and powers and made a public spectacle of them, triumphing over them by the cross. He elaborates even further in Ephesians 1:19–23 (NIV) when he states that God raised Christ from the dead and seated Him at His right hand in the heavenly realms, "far above all rule and authority, power and dominion, and every name that is invoked, not only in the present age but also in the one to come. And God placed all things under his feet and appointed him to be head over everything for the church, which is his body. . . ."

———— 6 ————

Other Old Testament scriptures spoke of defeating Edom and Moab. For example, see Psalm 60:8 and Isaiah 63:1–4. Psalm 83:3-8 talks about the various nations, including Edom and Moab, forming an alliance and plotting against Israel to destroy them.

The ultimate fulfillment of this prophecy occurred with the coming of God's own Son, Jesus. Like David, He descended from the lineage of Judah. His kingdom, however, would not be an earthly one, and the enemies He defeated would not be physical adversaries. Rather, His victory would be on a higher level—His kingdom would be a spiritual kingdom, and His reign would be eternal.[5] While He did not engage in physical battle with Moab and Edom, He defeated the forces of evil that these age-old enemies had come to symbolize for the Israelites.[6]

At Jesus's birth, a star in the east guided the magi to Bethlehem to pay tribute to Him. As a direct descendant of King David, He was the fulfillment of a promise God had made to David centuries earlier: "Your house and your kingdom will endure forever before me; your throne will be established forever" (2 Samuel 7:16, NIV). Thus, with the establishment of Christ's kingdom, the scepter of David passed eternally to Him.

Who would have thought that an ancient prophecy spoken by a soothsayer could be of such importance to us living today?

The kingdom God established through Christ Jesus is open to all peoples on earth, without regard to gender, race, nationality, or lineage.[7] Those who follow Jesus, trusting Him as their Savior and honoring Him as Lord, have been, and continue to be, the direct beneficiaries of that spiritual kingdom. The prophecy of the star and the scepter, spoken so long ago, continues to reach through the centuries and provide eternal hope for God's people.

> The kingdom God established through Christ Jesus is open to all peoples on earth, without regard to gender, race, nationality, or lineage.

"Where is he that is born King of the Jews? for we have seen his star in the east, and are come to worship him."

—Matthew 2:2, KJV

God Turns against Moab

We aren't told the timing of the oracles of Balaam, only that they occurred while the Israelites were camped on the plains of Moab. However, it's possible that at around the same time God was blessing the Israelites through Balaam's oracles, the people had already begun engaging in their atrocious behavior recorded in chapter 25.

Whatever the timing, God turned sharply against the Moabites after having protected their land all during the Israelites' journey. In this fourth oracle, He talked of crushing the skull of Moab (Numbers 24:17). He also declared in Deuteronomy 23:3–6 that neither the Moabites nor the Ammonites were to be allowed into the assembly of the Lord. Not only were they inhospitable toward the Israelites and failed to meet them with food and water on their way out of Egypt, but even worse, they hired Balaam to curse His people. He went on to state, "You shall not seek their peace nor their prosperity all your days forever" (Deuteronomy 23:6, NKJV).

As the Apostle Paul explains in Galatians 3:26–29 (NIV): "So in Christ Jesus you are all children of God through faith, for all of you who were baptized into Christ have clothed yourselves with Christ. There is neither Jew nor Gentile, neither slave nor free, nor is there male and female, for you are all one in Christ Jesus. If you belong to Christ, then you are Abraham's seed, and heirs according to the promise."

Thoughts to Ponder

In what ways do Moab and Edom represent evil? How can they be seen as adversaries of the church which Christ established?

_____

_____

_____

_____

In Acts 13:16–26, the Apostle Paul gives a brief summary of the history of Israel in which he explains the connection between King David and Jesus, the Messiah. Then, a few verses later, in Acts 13: 32–37, Paul goes on to state that Jesus fulfilled the promise God made to David. What contrast does he make between David and Jesus in verses 36–37? What is the difference between their kingdoms?

_____

_____

_____

_____

How were stars used in ancient times (and still today, on occasion)? How was the star a fitting symbol for the Messiah? How can we be like stars today? (See Philippians 2:15 and Daniel 12:3.)

_____

_____

_____

_____

Chapter 7

The Final Three Oracles of Balaam

Numbers 24:20–25, BSB

(20) Then Balaam saw Amalek and lifted up an oracle, saying:

"Amalek was first among the nations, but his end is destruction."

(21) Next he saw the Kenites and lifted up an oracle, saying:

"Your dwelling place is secure, and your nest is set in a cliff.

(22) Yet Kain will be destroyed when Asshur takes you captive."

(23) Once more Balaam lifted up an oracle, saying:

"Ah, who can live unless God has ordained it?

(24) Ships will come from the coasts of Cyprus; they will subdue Asshur and Eber, but they too will perish forever."

(25) Then Balaam arose and returned to his homeland, and Balak also went on his way.

◇◇◇

After foretelling the doom awaiting Moab and Edom, God turned His attention to other nations. Continuing to speak through Balaam, He presented three more short oracles.

Suggested Song

"I Stand in Awe of You"
(tinyurl.com/366e62t9)

——— 1 ———

The genealogy of Amalek is given in Genesis 36:9–12. Esau's son by his wife Adah was Eliphaz; no other sons by this wife are listed. Eliphaz had five sons, evidently by an unnamed wife, and one son, Amalek, by his concubine, Timna. Amalek is named as one of the chiefs among Esau's descendants in Genesis 36:15–16.

——— 2 ———

The account of the Israelites' battle with the Amalekites at Rephidim is given in Exodus 17:8–16.

——— 3 ———

As the Israelites were about to enter Canaan, Moses reminded the Israelites of what the Amalekites had done, saying, "When the LORD your God gives you rest from all the enemies around you in the land he is giving you to possess as an inheritance, you shall blot out the name of Amalek from under heaven. Do not forget!" (Deuteronomy 25:19, NIV).

The Destruction of Amalek

The first of these brief prophecies was a restatement of God's promise to destroy the Amalekites, who had earned the distinction of being the first nation to attack the Israelites as they journeyed from Egypt to the Promised Land.

Like the nations God had already cursed, the Amalekites were kinsmen of the Israelites (Amalek, a grandson of Esau, came from the land of Edom).[1] But unlike the Israelites, the Amalekites had no regard for God, much less His people. They demonstrated this by attacking the Israelites while they were camped at Rephidim, where God had supplied them with water from the rock at Horeb.

Moses described their cowardly act in Deuteronomy 25:17–18 (NKJV): "Remember what Amalek did to you on the way as you were coming out of Egypt, how he met you on the way and attacked your rear ranks, all the stragglers at your rear, when you were tired and weary; and he did not fear God."

Led into battle by Joshua, the Israelites retaliated. While Joshua and his men fought, Moses stood on a hill overlooking the battle. Moses lifted his hands toward heaven, raising his staff high—the same staff God had used to part the Red Sea. As long as Moses's hands were raised, the Israelites were successful, but when he lowered his hands, the Amalekites prevailed. As the battle waged on and Moses's strength weakened, Aaron and Hur found a rock for Moses to sit upon and then stood on either side of him for support. They held up Moses's hands, and eventually Joshua and the Israelites gained the victory over the Amalekites.[2]

When the battle ended, God gave Moses a message and told him to write it down—and to make sure Joshua heard it. God's decree was this: He would "utterly blot out the remembrance of Amalek from under heaven" (Exodus 17:14b, NKJV). In acknowledging their victory and God's promise, Moses built an altar there and called it, "The LORD is my banner." He went on to state, "They have raised their fist against the LORD's throne, so now the LORD will be at war with Amalek generation after generation" (Exodus 17:16, NLT).[3]

This short oracle reaffirmed God's intention to wipe out the Amalekites. He had not forgotten His decree or the treachery the Amalekites had inflicted upon His people.[4]

A Warning for the Kenites

The next group of people mentioned in Balaam's oracle were the Kenites, and it seems to be more of a warning concerning what would occur in the future rather than a curse.

Like the Israelites, the Kenites were descendants of Abraham. Although their land was included in what God promised to Abraham,[5] at least some of them gained favor with the Israelites. Moses's wife and his father-in-law were Kenites,[6] and Moses invited their family to the Promised Land.[7] "If you come with us, we will share with you whatever good things the LORD gives us," Moses told Hobab, his brother-in-law (Numbers 10:32, NIV).

In this second short oracle, God foretells of the captivity of the Kenites at the hands of Asshur (another name for Assyria).[8] It's likely that during the years Assyria conquered the Israelites, at least some of the Kenites were taken into captivity as well.[9]

Looking Further into the Future

The final short oracle of Balaam dealt with events that would occur centuries later. Ships would come from across the Mediterranean Sea to attack the whole region. Both the Assyrians (Asshur) and the Hebrews (Eber) would be subdued. Through the centuries, several invaders would indeed cross over, including Alexander the Great, as well as the Greeks and Romans.[10]

It might be worth noting here that throughout the Bible, God has used prophecies both as promises and as warnings. Sometimes a prophecy, like that of the Star and the King (who

—— 4 ——

Several centuries later, God charged King Saul to carry out the destruction of the Amalekites. Unfortunately, his failure to fulfill God's mandate completely led to his downfall as a king. See 1 Samuel 15 for this account.

—— 5 ——

See Genesis 15:18–21 for a listing of the land God promised to Abraham's descendants.

—— 6 ——

Moses's father-in-law, Jethro (also called Reuel), was a priest of Midian (Exodus 3:1). He gave Moses his daughter, Zipporah, to be his wife (Exodus 2:21). Later, as the Israelites were conquering the land of Canaan, Moses's father-in-law was referred to as a Kenite (Judges 1:16). The Kenites were a branch of the Midianites.

—— 7 ——

See Numbers 10:29–32 for Moses's invitation to Hobab, his brother-in-law, to accompany them. Hobab knew the area and served as a scout for the Israelites during their travels (verse 31). Hobab initially declined Moses's invitation, but it's likely he did accompany them. Later scriptures tell of Kenites who were Jethro's descendants that had traveled with the Israelites and went up from Jericho to live among the people of Judah (Judges 1:16 and Judges 4:11).

———— 8 ————

The mention of "Kain" evidently refers to the Kenites or the forefather of these people.

———— 9 ————

This article discusses the conquest of Israel by the Assyrians: "When and how was Israel conquered by the Assyrians?" (tinyurl. com/yc349sk8).

———— 10 ————

For more information concerning this oracle in Numbers 24:24, see *John Gill's Exposition of the Bible* (tinyurl.com/53rbjcrp) and the commentaries page at BibleHub.com (tinyurl.com/jmbcfvea).

———— 11 ————

See Deuteronomy 18:9–14 for the complete warning Moses gave the

would arise from Jacob's lineage), happened many years later. Sometimes the fruition was much more immediate. In every instance, what God said would happen actually happened, further confirming the power and omniscience of the One True God.

Balaam told Balak in Numbers 23:19 that God is not a man that he should lie— He will always make good on His promises. That was bad news for Balak, but it is wonderful news for those who continue to trust in the promises of God today.

> In every instance, what God said would happen actually happened, further confirming the power and omniscience of the One True God.

Revealing the Future to a Pagan by Means of a Pagan

Balaam's oracles are remarkable for several reasons. In most instances in the Bible, prophetic declarations were made by people who worshipped and followed God. Think of Elijah, Elisha, Jeremiah, and Isaiah, to name a few. Balaam, even though he served as God's mouthpiece, was not a follower of God but a soothsayer. Balaam practiced a form of magic arts or witchcraft and was known for casting curses. The Israelites had been strictly warned against engaging in such activities. In fact, Moses told them in Deuteronomy 18:12 (NIV), "Anyone who does these things is detestable to the LORD."[11]

Not only did God bestow blessings upon His people and reveal the future through this pagan soothsayer, but He did so in response to a pagan king. God told Balak what would become of various nations, including his own country of Moab. More surprising still, He chose this opportunity to tell of the coming of Christ. From the very people whom Balak had sought to harm would arise a Star who would become the ultimate ruler.

A Warning and Promise for Us

Balaam spoke directly with God, but he did not know Him. Unlike we do today, he did not have the written Word of God that allows us to understand God's character and His might. Through the Bible, we can learn about and, more importantly, learn from others' mistakes—mistakes like those that Balaam and Balak made in challenging God.

Today, we have the benefit of living on the other side of the cross, and we have the power of God's Spirit. God has made His plan of salvation clear in His Word. Through Jesus, His Son, He has expressed His great love for us. And in giving us His Spirit, God's presence lives in us.

If Balaam had been able to access all the knowledge that's available to us today, would he have changed his ways? That's something we cannot answer, but as for us, we can certainly learn from him. He serves as a prime example of things *not* to do. He also showed us that it avails us nothing to proclaim God's Word with our lips if we don't believe it in our hearts and practice it in our lives.

Israelites concerning these detestable practices.

For great is the LORD, and greatly to be praised, and he is to be feared above all gods. For all the gods of the peoples are worthless idols, but the LORD made the heavens.

—1 Chronicles 16:25–26, ESV

Thoughts to Ponder

Centuries later, God revealed the future kingdoms of the world to another pagan king, Nebuchadnezzar, who carried the Israelites off into Babylonian captivity. In his dream, how was the coming of Christ described? Read the account of Nebuchadnezzar's dream in Daniel 2. This article discusses the dream: "What is the meaning of Nebuchadnezzar's dream in Daniel 2?" (tinyurl.com/yjmyzfsc).

_____

_____

_____

_____

God can work through anyone He chooses. That does not mean, however, that God endorses or approves of that person. How did God work through Pharaoh when delivering the Israelites from Egyptian slavery? (See Exodus 9:16 and Romans 9:17.)

_____

_____

_____

_____

A little later in the history of the Israelites, Ruth from the land of Moab will come with her mother-in-law, Naomi, to live in Israel. What part does she play in the coming of Christ? What does her life say about the inclination of a person's heart versus his or her heritage? See the book of Ruth for her story. Ruth 4:13–22 gives the lineage which came from her.

_____

_____

_____

_____

ISRAEL SINS

Chapter 8

The Seduction of Israel

Numbers 25, BSB

(1) While Israel was staying in Shittim, the men began to indulge in sexual immorality with the daughters of Moab, (2) who also invited them to the sacrifices for their gods. And the people ate and bowed down to these gods. (3) So Israel joined in worshiping Baal of Peor, and the anger of the LORD burned against them.

(4) Then the LORD said to Moses, "Take all the leaders of the people and execute them in broad daylight before the LORD, so that His fierce anger may turn away from Israel."

(5) So Moses told the judges of Israel, "Each of you must kill all of his men who have joined in worshiping Baal of Peor."

(6) Just then an Israelite man brought to his family a Midianite woman in the sight of Moses and the whole congregation of Israel while they were weeping at the entrance to the Tent of Meeting. (7) On seeing this, Phinehas son of Eleazar, the son of Aaron the priest, got up from the assembly, took a spear in his hand, (8) followed the Israelite into his tent, and drove the spear through both of them—through the Israelite and on through the belly of the woman.

So the plague against the Israelites was halted, (9) but those who died in the plague numbered 24,000.

(10) Then the LORD said to Moses, (11) "Phinehas son of Eleazar, the son of Aaron the priest, has turned My wrath away from the Israelites; for he was zealous for My sake among them, so that I did not consume the Israelites in My zeal. (12) Declare, therefore, that I am granting him My covenant of peace. (13) It will be a covenant of permanent priesthood for him and his descendants, because he was zealous for his God and made atonement for the Israelites."

(14) The name of the Israelite who was slain with the Midianite woman was Zimri son of Salu, the leader of a Simeonite family. (15) And the name of the slain Midianite woman was Cozbi, the daughter of Zur, a tribal chief of a Midianite family.

(16) And the LORD said to Moses, (17) "Attack the Midianites and strike them dead. (18) For they assailed you deceitfully when they seduced you in the matter of Peor and their sister Cozbi, the daughter of the Midianite leader, the woman who was killed on the day the plague came because of Peor."

◇◇◇

Suggested Song

"Turn Your Eyes Upon Jesus" (tinyurl.com/23rhhvnc)

——— 1 ———

Shittim is short for Abel-Shittim and was named for the grove of acacia trees that grew on the eastern side of the Jordan River. Shittim served as Joshua's base camp before entering Canaan, and it was from there he sent spies over into Jericho (Joshua 2:1). A listing of the places where the Israelites camped along their forty-year journey is given in Numbers 33. Although their encampment here on the plains of Moab was the last stop Moses recorded in Numbers 33:48–49, Joshua tells us they left this camp at Shittim and camped on the river for three days before crossing on over (Joshua 3:1–2).

When the Israelites arrived at the plains of Moab, they had essentially reached the end of their arduous forty-year journey from Egypt. Their encampment stretched from Beth Jeshimoth to Abel Shittim, and Canaan lay just across the Jordan River.[1]

They stayed in this camp in Moab for at least two months.[2] All the happenings with Balaam and his oracles occurred during this time, as did the events in this chapter.

With their prize in sight, you would think nothing could divert the focus of the Israelites. They had just completed what amounted to a four-decade death sentence. The older generation had been condemned to die in the wilderness, which meant the younger generation had no choice but to trudge alongside their elders all those years. Both generations suffered because the older generation had lacked the faith to cross over and take the Promised Land as God had instructed them to do.[3]

> With their prize in sight, you would think nothing could divert the focus of the Israelites.

Consider for a moment the differences between the older and younger generations of the Israelites. The older ones had been born and raised in Egypt, immersed in a culture that worshipped a multitude of false gods. Their knowledge of the one true God had been secondhand, passed down to them from their ancestors. After the time of Jacob and Joseph, Scripture does not record God making Himself known to any of His people again until several centuries later when Moses came on the scene.[4]

The younger generation came of age in much different circumstances. Some were likely born in Egypt and crossed the Red Sea as children. Others were born during the Israelites' time in the wilderness. In either case, they had grown up hearing about the mighty things God had done for them and witnessing at least some of His great power firsthand. God delivered His Law at Mount Sinai just a few months after the Israelites left Egypt,[5] so this generation had the privilege of living under God's Law for most, if not all, of their lives.

By the time the Israelites finally arrived at the plains of Moab, the older generation had already died in the wilderness.[6] That meant it was the younger generation who allowed themselves to be pulled into sin by the Moabite and Midianite women.

Can you imagine the pain this incident caused God and Moses alike? Here the Israelites stood on the cusp of fulfilling the promise God had made to Abraham centuries earlier, only to have certain members of the community commit unspeakable acts of immorality. Chief among their sins was the worship of Baal. They forsook God and bowed down to an idol. As one Bible commentator stated, they committed the double offense of idolatry and licentiousness.[7] And don't forget, it was during this same time period while they were staying here on the plains of Moab that God, through Balaam's oracles, had been heaping His blessings upon the Israelite people, foretelling of the defeat of their enemies, and revealing the coming of the Messiah.

It's no wonder God's anger burned against the people. He was so angry that He employed a dual approach in punishing the offenders. He ordered all those who were leaders in the worshipping of Baal to be killed and their bodies hung out in the sun.[8] He also caused a deadly plague to come upon the people.

At the pronouncement of God's swift and severe punishment, some of the Israelites wept at the entrance to the Tent of Meeting, either in repentance or in sorrow for the loss of life. While the people mourned with Moses and the priests, an Israelite man

——— 2 ———

From Deuteronomy 1:3, 34:8 and Joshua 4:19, 5:10, we can determine that it took Moses about a month to write Deuteronomy and another month for the Israelites to mourn his death. The Israelites then crossed over the Jordan on the tenth day of the first month of the next year and celebrated the Passover in Canaan, which began at twilight on the fourteenth day of the first month. (See Exodus 12 for God's instructions concerning Passover. Verses 6 and 18 name the fourteenth day of the month as the beginning of the celebration.)

——— 3 ———

Numbers 13 tells of the twelve spies who explored Canaan, and Numbers 14 tells how the Israelites rebelled against God and refused to enter Canaan. Moses prayed for them, and God forgave them. Nevertheless, He declared in Numbers 14:26–35 that no one twenty years or older who was counted in the first census, except for

Joshua and Caleb, would ever see Canaan. The Israelites then wandered in the desert for forty years—one year for each day the spies explored Canaan—until everyone died whom God had so designated.

─────── 4 ───────

God acted through Joseph by allowing him to interpret dreams divinely (Genesis 40 and 41). Later, after he was already in Egypt, God told his father, Jacob, to go on down to Egypt, that Joseph's own hand would close his eyes (Genesis 46:2–4). This is the last recorded time that God spoke with the Israelites. Moses's call to lead the Israelites occurred several centuries later in Exodus 3.

─────── 5 ───────

The Israelites arrived at the Desert of Sinai in the third month after they left Egypt (Exodus 19:1). Shortly thereafter, God delivered the Ten Commandments (Exodus 20) and the remainder of His commands and instructions.

walked past them, parading a Midianite woman into the camp. Outraged at the sight, Phinehas, the son of Eleazar the priest, grabbed his spear and followed the couple into the man's tent. There, Phinehas thrust his spear through both the Israelite man and the Midianite women.

Phinehas's action appeased God's anger. The plague ceased, but 24,000 people had already died. God told Moses, "Since he was as zealous for my honor among them as I am, I did not put an end to them in my zeal" (Numbers 25:11, NIV). With his actions, Phinehas made atonement for the Israelites and stopped God from killing any more of them. As a result, God granted him a covenant of peace. This covenant would be one of a lasting priesthood for Phinehas and his descendants.

The psalmist later wrote of what the Israelites had done during the incident at Peor (Psalm 106:28–31, HCSB):

> "They aligned themselves with Baal of Peor
> and ate sacrifices offered to lifeless gods.
> They provoked the LORD with their deeds,
> and a plague broke out against them.
> But Phinehas stood up and intervened,
> and the plague was stopped.
> It was credited to him as righteousness
> throughout all generations to come."

The name of the Israelite man whom Phinehas killed was Zimri, the son of Salu, who was the leader of a family from the tribe of Simeon. The name of the woman whom Zimri brought into the Israelite camp was Cozbi, the daughter of Zur, a tribal chief of a Midianite family. The importance of these names will be seen later when Moses fulfills what will be his last charge from God, to take vengeance on the Midianites for the part they played in leading the Israelites astray.

A Self-Imposed Curse

What King Balak had been powerless to do, the Israelites brought upon themselves. Balaam's oracles had directed blessings toward them, but the lusts they allowed to grow in their hearts had indeed cursed them. They diverted their focus from their goal. As a result, 24,000 people who were only a stone's throw away from entering the Promised Land lay dead instead.

When we read the account of this tragic incident, it is easy to chastise the Israelites—*they knew better!* But when temptations come at us in real-time, they're not always so easy to recognize—or to avoid. The things we know better than to engage in are sometimes the very sins that ensnare us.

Sin will always be present in this world, but thankfully, we don't have to face it alone. In James 4:7–8a (NKJV) we are told, "Therefore submit to God. Resist the devil and he will flee from you. Draw near to God and He will draw near to you."

Submit to God—Listen to Him and obey Him.

Resist the devil—Avoid putting yourself in situations where you know you'll be tempted to sin.

Draw near to God—Make it a practice to read and study your Bible. Let God's Word speak to you, and let its precepts and promises soak into your mind and your very being. And let prayer become as natural in your life as breathing.

He will draw near to you—God draws near to us in His Word, through prayer, and with His Holy Spirit.

When we keep our eyes on Jesus and our hearts focused on God's Word, it's so much easier to keep our feet on the right path. After all, eternity is only a stone's throw away.

———— 6 ————

If any men of the older generation were still alive at this time, it would have been very few. In the next chapter, Numbers 26, God instructed Moses and Eleazar to take a census. One of the purposes of this census was to certify that none of those whom God had condemned to die in the wilderness was still alive.

———— 7 ————

See the *Jamieson-Fausset-Brown Bible Commentary* at BibleHub.com. Scroll down to "Numbers 25:3" (tinyurl.com/2p92cdpy).

———— 8 ————

The verse being referred to, Numbers 25:4, reads differently in the various versions. See BibleHub.com to compare versions: tinyurl.com/4p4mc6yu. Evidently God wanted to make an example of those who had sinned so grievously. While at Bible Hub, read what commentators have to say about this execution: tinyurl.com/fw3atn6k.

Therefore, since we are surrounded by such a great cloud of witnesses, let us throw off everything that hinders and the sin that so easily entangles. And let us run with perseverance the race marked out for us, fixing our eyes on Jesus, the pioneer and perfecter of faith. For the joy set before him he endured the cross, scorning its shame, and sat down at the right hand of the throne of God.

—Hebrews 12:1–2, NIV

Moses's Last Days

You may have wondered what Moses was doing while the Israelites were camped on the plains of Moab and Balaam was uttering his oracles. Actually, he only had about a month in that location before his death. During that time, he had much to do:

- *He had a lot of writing to do.* He finished the book of Numbers, which contains the story of Balaam, and wrote all of Deuteronomy.
- *He had a lot of speaking to do.* Not only did he write Deuteronomy, but he spoke it as well. He reviewed the Israelites' forty-year journey and all that God had done for them. Then he repeated the Ten Commandments as well as all the statutes and ordinances that together comprised the Law. Moses spoke of what God would do for the Israelites in the future and ratified their covenant with Him.

- *He and Eleazar, the high priest, took the second census* (Numbers 26).
- *He oversaw the war with the Midianites* (Numbers 31).
- *He turned the leadership of the Israelites over to Joshua* (Deuteronomy 31:23).
- *He wrote the Song of Moses* and then spoke it in the hearing of all the assembly of Israel (Deuteronomy 31:30–32:47).
- *He blessed the tribes of Israel* (Deuteronomy 33).
- *He climbed Mount Nebo to the top of Pisgah,* where God gave him a bird's eye tour of Canaan. There he died, and God buried him in the land of Moab (Deuteronomy 34). Moses, the servant of the Lord, had accomplished what God had called him to do.

Thoughts to Ponder

What were the first two of God's Ten Commandments? What does it mean that God is a jealous God? See Exodus 20:1–6.

_____

_____

_____

_____

When was another time that the Israelites let their focus be diverted and worshipped a false god? What happened as a result? See Exodus 32.

_____

_____

_____

_____

The sins that the Israelites committed in Numbers 25 remind us that we often cause the greatest harm to ourselves. What did Jesus have to say about this in Matthew 15:1–20? (A parallel account is given in Mark 7:1–23.)

_____

_____

_____

_____

_____

Chapter 9

Taking Vengeance on the Midianites

Numbers 31:1–18 and Joshua 13:15–23, BSB

Numbers 31:1–18

(1) And the LORD said to Moses, (2) "Take vengeance on the Midianites for the Israelites. After that, you will be gathered to your people."

(3) So Moses told the people, "Arm some of your men for war, that they may go against the Midianites and execute the LORD's vengeance on them. (4) Send into battle a thousand men from each tribe of Israel."

(5) So a thousand men were recruited from each tribe of Israel—twelve thousand armed for war. (6) And Moses sent the thousand from each tribe into battle, along with Phinehas son of Eleazar the priest, who took with him the vessels of the sanctuary and the trumpets for signaling.

(7) Then they waged war against Midian, as the LORD had commanded Moses, and they killed every male. (8) Among the slain were Evi, Rekem, Zur, Hur, and Reba—the five kings of Midian. They also killed Balaam son of Beor with the sword.

(9) The Israelites captured the Midianite women and their children, and they plundered all their herds, flocks, and goods. (10) Then they burned all the cities where the Midianites had lived, as well as all their encampments, (11) and carried away all the plunder and spoils, both people and animals.

(12) They brought the captives, spoils, and plunder to Moses, to Eleazar the priest, and to the congregation of Israel at the camp on the plains of Moab, by the Jordan across from Jericho. (13) And Moses, Eleazar the priest, and all the leaders of the congregation went to meet them outside the camp.

(14) But Moses was angry with the officers of the army—the commanders of thousands and commanders of hundreds—who were returning from the battle. (15) "Have you spared all the women?" he asked them. (16) "Look, these women caused the sons of Israel, through the

counsel of Balaam, to turn unfaithfully against the LORD at Peor, so that the plague struck the congregation of the LORD. (17) So now, kill all the boys, as well as every woman who has had relations with a man, (18) but spare for yourselves every girl who has never had relations with a man.

Joshua 13:15–23

(15) This is what Moses had given to the clans of the tribe of Reuben:

(16) The territory from Aroer on the rim of the Arnon Valley, along with the city in the middle of the valley, to the whole plateau beyond Medeba, (17) to Heshbon and all its cities on the plateau, including Dibon, Bamoth-baal, Beth-baal-meon, (18) Jahaz, Kedemoth, Mephaath, (19) Kiriathaim, Sibmah, Zereth-shahar on the hill in the valley, (20) Beth-peor, the slopes of Pisgah, and Beth-jeshimoth—(21) all the cities of the plateau and all the kingdom of Sihon king of the Amorites, who reigned in Heshbon until Moses killed him and the chiefs of Midian (Evi, Rekem, Zur, Hur, and Reba), the princes of Sihon who lived in the land.

(22) The Israelites also killed the diviner Balaam son of Beor along with the others they put to the sword. (23) And the border of the Reubenites was the bank of the Jordan.

This was the inheritance of the clans of the Reubenites, including the cities and villages.

◇◇◇

Suggested Song

"Nothing But the Blood" (tinyurl.com/36jchc65)

——— 1 ———

See Numbers 20:2–13 for the account of Moses striking the rock to obtain water at Meribah rather than speaking to it as God had commanded.

——— 2 ———

See Numbers 20:22–29 for the account of Aaron's death on Mt. Hor. In Numbers 33:38–39, the

During their desert wanderings, Moses and Aaron sinned at Meribah when Moses struck the rock to bring forth water for the Israelites. As a result, God declared that neither of them would be allowed to cross over into Canaan.[1] Aaron had already died upon Mount Hor a few months earlier, and the office of high priest passed to his son, Eleazar.[2] Now, with the Israelites set to cross the Jordan River, Moses's time on earth was rapidly drawing to a close.

God had one last mission for Moses to accomplish before his death. He was to take vengeance on the Midianites. He had already told him the reason why: "Because they assaulted you with deceit and tricked you into worshipping Baal of Peor, and because of Cozbi, the daughter of a Midianite leader, who was killed at the time of the plague because of what happened at Peor" (Numbers 25:18, NLT).[3]

So the Israelites went to battle and killed the Midianite men, including five Midianite kings, one of whom was Zur, the father of Cozbi. They burned all the Midianite cities and encampments and took away as plunder the remainder of the people, along with their goods and animals. The Israelite officers even reported they lost none of their own men in the battle.[4]

Unfortunately, their victorious homecoming was short-lived. When Moses realized his officers had spared the Midianite women and children, he became angry. He ordered all the women and all the boys to be killed. Only the young girls could be allowed to live.

Moses then stated his reason for executing the women: "Look, these women caused the sons of Israel, through the counsel of Balaam, to turn unfaithfully against the LORD at Peor, so that the plague struck the congregation of the LORD" (Numbers 31:16, BSB). In all likelihood, some of these women had been among those who had sought to lead the men of Israel astray, resulting in the deaths of 24,000. It was their actions that had caused God to declare this war on the Midianites.

But why did Moses also condemn the boys while sparing the girls? Back in Numbers 25:17, God told Moses to treat the Midianites as enemies and to kill them. If Moses had spared the boys, then their family name and lineage would have continued. Females did not carry their family lineage, and because only those who were virgins were spared, they were not the ones who had engaged in immoral behavior with the Israelite men.[5]

No Match for God

The last we heard of Balaam, he was supposed to be headed back home.[6] Obviously he didn't make it. He is listed among the casualties of the war which the Israelites waged upon the Midianites.

Finally, here in Numbers 31, we learn the rest of the story about Balaam or, at least, the highlights. At some point, he

scriptures state Aaron died during the fortieth year after the Israelites came out of Egypt at the age of 123, so we know his death had occurred near the end of their journey.

——— 3 ———

It seems the Midianites were a nomadic people at this time and did not occupy a defined land, as did the Moabites. The Midianites upon whom God took vengeance evidently were the ones who lived among the Moabites or in that region who had engaged in the scheme to lure the Israelites into idolatry and immorality. The Midianites who lived among the Israelite community were not part of this group. You may recall that Moses's wife and family were Midianites, and after the Israelites entered Canaan, some of the descendants of Jethro, Moses's father-in-law, settled among the Israelites in Judah (Judges 1:16).

——— 4 ———

See Numbers 31:48–54 for the account of the Israelite officers reporting

———————— 5 ————————

These articles provide more insight on this subject: "Why were only the virgins left alive among the Midianites in Numbers 31:17-18?" (tinyurl.com/yyhtmhxk), and "Why did God command the Israelites to completely destroy the Midianites in Numbers 31:17?" (tinyurl.com/2p899pk8).

———————— 6 ————————

See Numbers 24:25. While it's possible Balaam went home and then came back to where he was killed, it seems unlikely due to the distance he would have had to travel.

———————— 7 ————————

Satan, likewise, understands human frailties. While he can't make us sin, he certainly knows what tempts us.

counseled the Midianites and the Moabites concerning the Israelites' vulnerabilities. He knew that any attempt to curse the Israelites would prove futile. God could protect His people from outside sources, but what God couldn't protect them against was themselves.

The scriptures tell us in Revelation 2:14 (NIV) that Balaam "taught Balak to entice the Israelites to sin so that they ate food sacrificed to idols and committed sexual immorality." Balaam knew if they were tempted with sensual pleasures, at least some of them would succumb. He certainly understood human nature and human frailties.[7]

Balaam also knew from his oracles that God was powerful, and he knew how much God loved and cared for the Israelites. But somehow Balaam thought he could do an end run around God. He attempted to double around behind God's back to bring about the curse on the Israelites that Balak had sought. He learned too late that his deviousness was no match for God.

Why would Balaam do this? The New Testament provides more insight into his motive. Jude warned about ungodly people who "have rushed for profit into Balaam's error" (Jude 1:11, NIV). The Apostle Peter had this to say concerning false prophets in 2 Peter 2:15–16 (BSB): "They have left the straight way and wandered off to follow the way of Balaam son of Beor, who loved the wages of wickedness. But he was rebuked for his transgression by a donkey, otherwise without speech, that spoke with a man's voice and restrained the prophet's madness."

Did you notice the words "profit" and "wages" in the above passages? Balaam was accustomed to being paid for his services. Being sent home empty-handed would have been an embarrassment and reflected poorly on his ability as a soothsayer. He knew that King Balak was willing to reward him handsomely, if only he could accomplish what he had been asked to do—to curse the Israelites.

In the end, Balaam's desire for money outweighed his fear of God. He wanted to profit from this situation, and the fact that people were likely to be hurt or killed in the process didn't seem to bother him. Balaam made a fatal mistake—he misjudged God's reach and power. God did not let him get away with his treachery. Balaam had little time to enjoy his ill-gotten gain before he was killed. And it's quite likely that upon his death, his money was taken by the Israelite soldiers as plunder of the war. Certainly, he did not die the death of the righteous that he spoke of in Numbers 23:10.

> In the end, Balaam's desire for money outweighed his fear of God.

Think of all the pain this incident caused. The Israelites who sinned forsook the God who had delivered them from Egyptian slavery. They had violated His Laws with their vile behavior and worshipped a pagan god. They abandoned their leader, Moses, who had struggled during the last forty years of his life to deliver them to the Promised Land. And they irreparably damaged their families, who were left to continue without them.

Think of the pain we cause today when we sin: to our God who created us, to Jesus who gave His life for us, and to our loved ones who depend on us. Sin separates us from God, but thanks be to Jesus for His great sacrifice. His blood takes our sin away. Because of Him, we can receive forgiveness. Because of Him, we can look forward to a Promised Land much greater than Canaan. We can look forward to heaven and an eternity with God!

What Happened to King Balak and the Land of Moab?

The last time we heard of Balak was in Numbers 24:25 (NIV) after all the oracles had ended: "Then Balaam got up and returned home, and Balak went his own way." It's quite possible Balak was killed when the Israelites went to battle against the Midianites, and his name wasn't recorded. Or he simply could have faded into obscurity. The Bible doesn't tell us what happened to him.

We do know that at least some of the land of Moab was claimed by the Israelites. Moses awarded land east of the Jordan to the tribes of Reuben, Gad, and the half tribe of Manasseh. The reading for this lesson includes a passage from Joshua 13, which describes the boundaries of the land Moses awarded to the tribe of Reuben. You may recognize in verse 20 the names of Beth Peor, the slopes of Pisgah, and Beth Jeshimoth from other readings.

The Israelites' camp on the plains of Moab

stretched from Beth Jeshimoth to Abel Shittim (Numbers 33:49). The mountain peak of Pisgah was one of the sites where Balaam had Balak build seven altars (Numbers 23:14). It was also where God allowed Moses to look over into the land of Canaan shortly before his death (Deuteronomy 34:1). And because Moses could not cross over into Canaan, God buried him in Moab, in the valley opposite Beth Peor (Deuteronomy 34:5–6).

Consequently, just as one trespass resulted in condemnation for all people, so also one righteous act resulted in justification and life for all people.

—Romans 5:18, NIV

Thoughts to Ponder

The Israelites had lived apart from other people since they left Egypt. What do you think it was like for them when they arrived on the plains of Moab with all these other people and gods? What did God instruct them to do when they entered Canaan? See Deuteronomy 7:1–6.

_____

_____

_____

_____

The king of Moab was the one who had initially sought to have the Israelites cursed. Yet, God did not declare war upon the Moabites as he did the Midianites. In what other ways did God punish the Moabites? See Deuteronomy 23:3–6.

_____

_____

_____

_____

Did Moses and the Israelites know at the time it was happening that Balak was trying to curse them? Did they know about Balaam's oracles concerning them? If they had known about the oracles, do you think they would have stood any stronger against the temptations presented to them? When you know that someone else loves you and has great confidence in you, how does that help you meet life's challenges?

_____

_____

_____

_____

Chapter 10

Wrapping It Up: The Second Census

Numbers 26, BSB

[*Note*: It can be tempting to scan through or skip a long list of hard-to-pronounce names in the Bible. It's interesting here, however, to see those you may recognize from other readings.]

(1) After the plague had ended, the LORD said to Moses and Eleazar son of Aaron the priest, (2) "Take a census of the whole congregation of Israel by the houses of their fathers—all those twenty years of age or older who can serve in the army of Israel."

(3) So on the plains of Moab by the Jordan, across from Jericho, Moses and Eleazar the priest issued the instruction, (4) "Take a census of the men twenty years of age or older, as the LORD has commanded Moses."

And these were the Israelites who came out of the land of Egypt:

The Tribe of Reuben

(5) Reuben was the firstborn of Israel. These were the descendants Reuben:

The Hanochite clan from Hanoch, the Palluite clan from Pallu,

(6) the Hezronite clan from Hezron, and the Carmite clan from Carmi.

(7) These were the clans of Reuben, and their registration numbered 43,730.

(8) Now the son of Pallu was Eliab, (9) and the sons of Eliab were Nemuel, Dathan, and Abiram.

It was Dathan and Abiram, chosen by the congregation, who fought against Moses and Aaron with the followers of Korah who rebelled against the LORD. (10) And the earth opened its mouth and swallowed them along with Korah, whose followers died when the fire consumed 250 men. They serve as a warning sign. (11) However, the line of Korah did not die out.

The Tribe of Simeon

(12) These were the descendants of Simeon by their clans:

The Nemuelite clan from Nemuel,
the Jaminite clan from Jamin,
the Jachinite clan from Jachin,

(13) the Zerahite clan from Zerah,
and the Shaulite clan from Shaul.

(14) These were the clans of Simeon, and there were 22,200 men.

The Tribe of Gad

(15) These were the descendants of Gad by their clans:

The Zephonite clan from Zephon,
the Haggite clan from Haggi,
the Shunite clan from Shuni,

(16) the Oznite clan from Ozni,
the Erite clan from Eri,

(17) the Arodite clan from Arod,
and the Arelite clan from Areli.

(18) These were the clans of Gad, and their registration numbered 40,500.

The Tribe of Judah

(19) The sons of Judah were Er and Onan, but they died in the land of Canaan. (20) These were the descendants of Judah by their clans:

The Shelanite clan from Shelah,
the Perezite clan from Perez,
and the Zerahite clan from Zerah.

(21) And these were the descendants of Perez:

the Hezronite clan from Hezron
and the Hamulite clan from Hamul.

(22) These were the clans of Judah, and their registration numbered 76,500.

The Tribe of Issachar

(23) These were the descendants of Issachar by their clans:

The Tolaite clan from Tola,
the Punite clan from Puvah,

(24) the Jashubite clan from Jashub,
and the Shimronite clan from Shimron.

(25) These were the clans of Issachar, and their registration numbered 64,300.

The Tribe of Zebulun

(26) These were the descendants of Zebulun by their clans:

The Seredite clan from Sered,
the Elonite clan from Elon,
and the Jahleelite clan from Jahleel.

(27) These were the clans of Zebulun, and their registration numbered 60,500.

The Tribe of Manasseh

(28) The descendants of Joseph included the clans of Manasseh and Ephraim.

(29) These were the descendants of Manasseh:

The Machirite clan from Machir, the father of Gilead, and the Gileadite clan from Gilead.

(30) These were the descendants of Gilead:

the Iezerite clan from Iezer,
the Helekite clan from Helek,

(31) the Asrielite clan from Asriel,
the Shechemite clan from Shechem,

(32) the Shemidaite clan from Shemida,
and the Hepherite clan from Hepher.

(33) Now Zelophehad son of Hepher had
no sons but only daughters. The names of
his daughters were Mahlah, Noah, Hoglah,
Milcah, and Tirzah.

(34) These were the clans of Manasseh, and
their registration numbered 52,700.

The Tribe of Ephraim

(35) These were the descendants of Ephraim
by their clans:

The Shuthelahite clan from Shuthelah,
the Becherite clan from Becher,
and the Tahanite clan from Tahan.

(36) And the descendants of Shuthelah
were the Eranite clan from Eran.

(37) These were the clans of Ephraim, and
their registration numbered 32,500.

These clans were the descendants of Joseph.

The Tribe of Benjamin

(38) These were the descendants of Benjamin
by their clans:

The Belaite clan from Bela,
the Ashbelite clan from Ashbel,
the Ahiramite clan from Ahiram,

(39) the Shuphamite clan from Shupham,
and the Huphamite clan from Hupham.

(40) And the descendants of Bela from Ard
and Naaman were the Ardite clan from
Ard and the Naamite clan from Naaman.

(41) These were the clans of Benjamin, and
their registration numbered 45,600.

The Tribe of Dan

(42) These were the descendants of Dan by
their clans:

The Shuhamite clan from Shuham.

These were the clans of Dan. (43) All of them
were Shuhamite clans, and their registration
numbered 64,400.

The Tribe of Asher

(44) These were the descendants of Asher by
their clans:

The Imnite clan from Imnah,
the Ishvite clan from Ishvi,
and the Beriite clan from Beriah.

(45) And these were the descendants of
Beriah:

the Heberite clan from Heber
and the Malchielite clan from Malchiel.

(46) And the name of Asher's daughter
was Serah.

(47) These were the clans of Asher, and their
registration numbered 53,400.

The Tribe of Naphtali

(48) These were the descendants of Naphtali
by their clans:

The Jahzeelite clan from Jahzeel,
the Gunite clan from Guni,

(49) the Jezerite clan from Jezer,
and the Shillemite clan from Shillem.

(50) These were the clans of Naphtali, and their registration numbered 45,400.

(51) These men of Israel numbered 601,730 in all.

Inheritance by Lot

(52) Then the LORD said to Moses, (53) "The land is to be divided among the tribes as an inheritance, according to the number of names. (54) Increase the inheritance for a large tribe and decrease it for a small one; each tribe is to receive its inheritance according to the number of those registered.

(55) Indeed, the land must be divided by lot; they shall receive their inheritance according to the names of the tribes of their fathers. (56) Each inheritance is to be divided by lot among the larger and smaller tribes."

The Levites Numbered

(57) Now these were the Levites numbered by their clans:

> The Gershonite clan from Gershon,
> the Kohathite clan from Kohath,
> and the Merarite clan from Merari.

(58) These were the families of the Levites:

> The Libnite clan,
> the Hebronite clan,
> the Mahlite clan,
> the Mushite clan,
> and the Korahite clan.

Now Kohath was the father of Amram, (59) and Amram's wife was named Jochebed. She was also a daughter of Levi, born to Levi in Egypt. To Amram she bore Aaron, Moses, and their sister Miriam. (60) Nadab, Abihu, Eleazar, and Ithamar were born to Aaron, (61) but Nadab and Abihu died when they offered unauthorized fire before the LORD.

(62) The registration of the Levites totaled 23,000, every male a month old or more; they were not numbered among the other Israelites, because no inheritance was given to them among the Israelites.

Only Caleb and Joshua Remain

(63) These were the ones numbered by Moses and Eleazar the priest when they counted the Israelites on the plains of Moab by the Jordan, across from Jericho.

(64) Among all these, however, there was not one who had been numbered by Moses and Aaron the priest when they counted the Israelites in the Wilderness of Sinai. (65) For the LORD had told them that they would surely die in the wilderness. Not one was left except Caleb son of Jephunneh and Joshua son of Nun.

◇◇◇

The Count of the Twelve Tribes of Israel

The chart below compares the numbers of those counted in the twelve tribes of Israel in the first and second censuses, as well as the difference between the two counts. Only men who were twenty or older and able to serve in the army of Israel were counted. Men from the tribe of Levi were not included in these censuses and did not serve in the army. They were numbered separately, with all their males age one month and older being counted. (See Numbers 1 for the actual number of men counted in Census 1, with the criteria for counting them given in verses 2–3. For Levi, see Numbers 3:15, 39. For Census 2, see Numbers 26, with the count for Levi given in verse 62.)

Tribe	1st Census- Numbers 1	2nd Census- Numbers 26	Difference
Reuben	46,500	43,730	-2,770
Simeon	59,300	22,200	-37,100
Gad	45,650	40,500	-5,150
Judah	74,600	76,500	1,900
Issachar	54,400	64,300	9,900
Zebulun	57,400	60,500	3,100
Manasseh	32,200	52,700	20,500
Ephraim	40,500	32,500	-8,000
Benjamin	35,400	45,600	10,200
Dan	62,700	64,400	1,700
Asher	41,500	53,400	11,900
Naphtali	53,400	45,400	-8,000
Total	603,550	601,730	-1,820
Levi	22,000	23,000	1,000

About a year after the Israelites left Egypt, God instructed Moses to take the first census of the Israelite community while they were camped in the Wilderness of Sinai. He and his brother Aaron, who was the high priest, were to count and list by name

"To Canaan's Land I'm on My Way!" (tinyurl.com/2tj2cfnf)

Who Were the Twelve Tribes of Israel?

Joseph and Levi were both sons of Jacob (Israel); however, their names are not listed among the twelve tribes of Israel.

God set apart the tribe of Levi for His service. While they did not receive a land allotment in Canaan like the other tribes, God did provide for their needs. They received the tithes the Israelites offered, as well as portions of various sacrifices. They were also allotted cities in which to live, which were dispersed throughout the twelve tribes.[1]

So, what about Joseph? As Jacob's favorite son, he should have had a place among the twelve tribes. And he did, not by his name but by his sons, Ephraim and Manasseh.

Here's how Joseph's descendants became two separate tribes. Joseph was born as the first son to Rachel, the wife whom Jacob chose and the woman he loved. Jacob favored Joseph to the point that his brothers hated him and sold him into slavery. God watched over Joseph and brought him from slavery to second-in-command in Egypt.

For many years, Jacob believed that Joseph had been killed as a young man, which was the story Joseph's older brothers told their father. Imagine his joy when Jacob learned that Joseph was still alive! God then promised Jacob that Joseph's own hand would close his eyes (meaning he would be with him at his death).

Joseph's high rank allowed him to move his entire family from famine-weary Canaan to Egypt, where the food was plentiful. There, with all his family around him, Jacob enjoyed the last seventeen years of his life. Before his death, Jacob blessed Joseph's two sons, Ephraim and Manasseh, and declared they would be considered as his own children. That meant they would each

all the men who were age twenty or older and were able to serve in the army. These men were to be the ones who would fight for Israel when called upon.[2]

This census did not include women, and it evidently did not include men who were considered unable to fight due to age or disabilities. Neither were the men from the tribe of Levi included in this census. God set them apart to serve as His priests and to care for the tabernacle. They did not fight in the army, nor did they receive an inheritance of land in Canaan. Rather, God served as their inheritance. They were counted separately and by different criteria. (For their tribe, all males age one month and older were counted.)[3]

The Israelites stayed encamped at Mount Sinai for almost a year. While there, God delivered to them the Ten Commandments and His Law. If all had gone smoothly, the Israelites would likely have entered Canaan fairly soon after leaving Mount Sinai. We know that because Deuteronomy 1:2 states it is an eleven-day journey from Horeb or Sinai to Kadesh-barnea, the place where Moses later sent the twelve men into Canaan to spy out the land.

These twelve Israelite men explored the land of Canaan and returned forty days later. They reported that, although this was a land of great abundance, the people were powerful, and their cities were fortified and very large. With their reports, ten of the spies instilled fear in the people and convinced them that the residents of Canaan would be too strong for them. Only two of the men, Joshua and Caleb, encouraged the people to take possession of the land.[4]

The people gave in to their fears and refused to cross into Canaan. They even talked about choosing a leader and going back to Egypt. When Joshua and Caleb encouraged them to go ahead and enter the land, the people talked of stoning them.

At that point, God wanted to destroy the Israelites for their lack of faith in Him, but Moses interceded on their behalf.

Although God forgave them, He declared that, except for Joshua and Caleb, no one who was twenty or older and had been counted in the first census would ever see or enter Canaan. He sentenced the Israelites to wander in the wilderness for forty years, one year for each day the spies had explored the land, until all those God had so designated had died.[5]

At the end of the forty years, the Israelites who had survived their journey arrived at Shittim, or the Acacia Grove, on the plains of Moab. Right across the Jordan River lay their goal. Unfortunately, one of the greatest challenges of their entire journey also lay there at the entrance to the Promised Land.

> Unfortunately, one of the greatest challenges of their entire journey also lay there at the entrance to the Promised Land.

Near the Israelites' encampment on the east side of the Jordan lay Peor, a place where the Moabites worshipped their false god, Baal. Their sacrificial events involved food, idol worship, and, of course, women. You can imagine that the sights, the sounds, the smells, the rituals—everything stood in stark contrast to the wilderness wanderings the Israelites had known their whole lives. Canaan was within reach, but 24,000 of them forfeited everything for a few moments of carnal pleasure.

The Importance of the Second Census

The reading for this chapter, Numbers 26, gives the account of the second census. By this time, the unfortunate incident of their engaging in vile behavior and Baal worship had ended, as had the plague that killed so many.

So there, on the plains of Moab by the Jordan River across from Jericho, the Lord commanded Moses and Eleazar (who was then the high priest) to take a second census of the Israelite community by families. As before, all the men age twenty and older who were able to serve in the army were counted, except for those from the tribe of Levi.

inherit territory along with the rest of Jacob's sons. In effect, this gave Joseph's offspring a double portion of Jacob's inheritance, and Ephraim and Manasseh's descendants each became a tribe of their own. (See Genesis 48:5–6 for the account of Jacob declaring that Ephraim and Manasseh were to be his.)

——— 1 ———

For more information about the cities allotted to the Levites, see "Levitical Cities" in the *Encyclopedia of the Bible* (tinyurl.com/mu6hucdr).

——— 2 ———

See Numbers 1 for the account of the first census. The explanation for who was to be counted is given in Numbers 1:2–3.

——— 3 ———

Numbers 1:47–53 list the Levites' responsibilities. In Numbers 3:11–13, God stated that the Levites were His. The explanation for how the Levite males were to be counted is given in Numbers 3:14–15. Concerning the land allotments, the

Israelites needed land for their livestock and crops so they could make a living off the land and feed their families. The men from the tribe of Levi spent much of their time and effort serving God, so they would have been at a great disadvantage if they also had to try to feed their families from the land. God provided for their needs by giving them the tithes (money) that the other Israelites offered to God (Numbers 18:20–24). They also received portions of certain sacrifices (food) that the Israelites offered. Additionally, God designated forty-eight cities where they could live throughout the other tribes, and surrounding each city was a portion of land set aside for their use. That way, their families had an area for a few animals and crops.

———— 4 ————

See Numbers 13 for the account of the twelve spies exploring the land of Canaan. In verse 30, Caleb encouraged the people to go ahead and take possession of the land. When the people began to rebel, both

The second census accomplished several things. With a count being taken of each tribe, it helped determine how the land of Canaan would be allotted. Each tribe was awarded a portion depending on its size, with the larger tribes receiving more land and the smaller tribes less.

This census also verified that all those men who had been counted in the first census and condemned to die in the wilderness were indeed dead. Of that group, only Joshua and Caleb remained. They were the two spies who knew that, with God's help, the Israelites would be able to claim the Promised Land.

The second census, in effect, cleared the way for the Israelites to cross over into Canaan. It also meant that Moses's job and life on earth had come to an end. And although God did not allow Moses to enter Canaan, He did give him a personal, bird's-eye tour from atop Mount Nebo.[6]

One of Moses's final acts on earth was to bless the tribes. As their leader, he had been much like a father to them, and to them he had devoted the last forty years of his life. In his blessings, Moses named every tribe but one—Simeon.[7] Bible scholars can only speculate as to why, but it's possible Moses omitted this tribe because of the role they played in the worship of Baal of Peor.

Zimri, the son of Salu, the leader of a Simeonite family, was the only Israelite specifically named in the incident at Peor, and the numbers from the second census show a dramatic drop for their tribe. In fact, their men were down by more than half. We know that 24,000 Israelites died from the plague that ensued because of their idol worship. It's quite possible that many of the offenders were from the tribe of Simeon, but the scriptures do not tell us this.

Keep Your Eyes on the Promises of God

God had protected the Israelites from outside forces in the wilderness for forty years, but as the story of Balaam illustrates so well, He could not protect them from the forces within.

God did not create humans to be pre-programmed robots. Rather, he granted us free will. Each of us must decide in our own hearts the direction we will take. The challenges that ultimately take us down are the ones that come from within.

No matter how long you may live on this earth, life is short and eternity is forever. It's unlikely there will ever be a time in your life that you don't face temptations. When you overcome one trial, sin simply repackages itself and comes at you from another angle.

> No matter how long you may live on this earth, life is short and eternity is forever.

Let the words in James 1:12 (NIV) encourage you as you face whatever may come your way: "Blessed is the one who perseveres under trial because, having stood the test, that person will receive the crown of life that the Lord has promised to those who love him."

Love the Lord and cling to His Word. For each of us, eternity is only a heartbeat away. Today and every day of our lives, we, like the Israelites, stand at the threshold. Our Promised Land, however, will be a glorious eternal home with Him! Don't let anything divert your focus.

Caleb and Joshua tried to reason with the people in Numbers 14:6-10. For doing so, the people talked of stoning them. God specifically stated both Caleb and Joshua would be allowed to enter Canaan in Numbers 14:30.

————— 5 —————

See Numbers 14 for the account of the people rebelling against God and refusing to enter Canaan. God made His pronouncement on them in Numbers 14:28–35 and 32:11–13.

————— 6 —————

The account of Moses's death is given in Deuteronomy 34.

————— 7 —————

See Deuteronomy 33 for Moses's blessings on the tribes.

Whoever sows to please their flesh, from the flesh will reap destruction; whoever sows to please the Spirit, from the Spirit will reap eternal life.

—Galatians 6:8, NIV

So we do not focus on what is seen, but on what is unseen. For what is seen is temporary, but what is unseen is eternal.

—2 Corinthians 4:18, HCSB

Thoughts to Ponder

Why were only the men who were counted in the first census the ones condemned to die in the wilderness during the forty years of wandering?

_____

_____

_____

_____

In the second census, several tribes saw a decline in their count as compared to the first census. What could have caused these tribes to have fewer men age twenty and over who were able to fight in the army in the second census? How many times during their wilderness journeys were people killed for their rebellion or disobedience? How did this affect their numbers in the second census?

_____

_____

_____

_____

When Jacob, or Israel, gave his blessings to his sons in Genesis 49:5–7, what did he say concerning Simeon and Levi? Why did he say this? (See Genesis 34.) How was his blessing fulfilled? (See Deuteronomy 18:1–2 and Joshua 19:1–9.) This article discusses "How was God Himself the inheritance of the Levites?" (tinyurl.com/59p52tz9).

_____

_____

_____

_____

"Beware of false prophets who come disguised as harmless sheep but are really vicious wolves. You can identify them by their fruit, that is, by the way they act.

"Can you pick grapes from thornbushes, or figs from thistles? A good tree produces good fruit, and a bad tree produces bad fruit. A good tree can't produce bad fruit, and a bad tree can't produce good fruit. So every tree that does not produce good fruit is chopped down and thrown into the fire.

"Yes, just as you can identify a tree by its fruit, so you can identify people by their actions."

—Matthew 7:15–20, NLT

Resources

Throughout this book, tiny URLs have been used to keep the text clean. The full links are provided here along with the resources cited.

Setting the Scene

Berean Standard Bible, https://berean.bible/downloads.htm.

Bible Hub, https://biblehub.com.

Chapter 1

[Sidebar] "Commentaries: Numbers 22:5," *Bible Hub*, https://biblehub.com/commentaries/numbers/22-5.htm.

Chapter 2

1. "Donkey Information Guide," *The Donkey Listener*, https://donkeylistener.com/donkey-information-guide.

1. Khadilkar, Dhananjay, "How Donkeys Changed the Course of Human History," *BBC.com*, January 16, 2023, https://www.bbc.com/future/article/20230116-how-donkeys-changed-the-course-of-human-history.

Chapter 3

2. "What is the significance of high places in the Bible?", *Got Questions Ministries*, accessed February 21, 2023, https://www.gotquestions.org/high-places.html.

2. "The Worship of Baal," *Bible History*, https://bible-history.com/resource/the-worship-of-baal.

Thoughts to Ponder, Question 1: Smyth, Dolores, "What Does the Number 7 Mean in the Bible and Why is it Important?", *Christianity.com*, July 11, 2023, https://www.christianity.com/wiki/bible/what-is-the-biblical-significance-of-the-number-7.html.

Chapter 4

Thoughts to Ponder, Question 1: "Numbers 23:21," *Bible Hub,* https://biblehub.com/numbers/23-21.htm.

Thoughts to Ponder, Question 1: "Commentaries: Numbers 23:21," *Bible Hub*, https://biblehub.com/commentaries/numbers/23-21.htm.

Thoughts to Ponder, Question 3: "Who/what is the Lion of the tribe of Judah?", *Got Questions Ministries*, accessed February 21, 2023, https://www.gotquestions.org/lion-tribe-Judah.html.

Thoughts to Ponder, Question 3: Haynes, Clarence L., Jr., "4 Powerful Reasons to Understand and Know Jesus as the Lion of Judah," *Bible Study Tools,* December 20, 2022, https://www.biblestudytools.com/bible-study/topical-studies/powerful-reasons-to-know-god-as-the-lion-of-judah.html.

Chapter 5

Thoughts to Ponder, Question 2: "Encampment of the Tribes of Israel in the Wilderness," *Conforming To Jesus Ministry*, https://www.conformingtojesus.com/charts-maps/en/wilderness_camp_of_the_tribes_of_israel.htm.

[Sidebar] "Pentateuch, The," *Smith's Bible Dictionary, Bible Study Tools*, https://www.biblestudytools.com/dictionaries/smiths-bible-dictionary/pentateuch-the.html.

[Sidebar] "Deuteronomy," *Easton's Bible Dictionary, Bible Study Tools,* https://www.biblestudytools.com/dictionaries/eastons-bible-dictionary/deuteronomy.html.

Chapter 7

9. "When and how was Israel conquered by the Assyrians?", *Got Questions Ministries*, accessed February 21, 2023, https://www.gotquestions.org/Israel-conquered-by-Assyria.html.

10. "Numbers 24:24," *John Gill's Exposition of the Bible, Bible Study Tools*, https://www.biblestudytools.com/commentaries/gills-exposition-of-the-bible/numbers-24-24.html.

10. "Commentaries: Numbers 24:24," *Bible Hub*, https://biblehub.com/commentaries/numbers/24-24.htm.

Thoughts to Ponder, Question 1: "What is the meaning of Nebuchadnezzar's dream in Daniel 2?", *Got Questions Ministries*, accessed February 21, 2023, https://www.gotquestions.org/nebuchadnezzars-dream.html.

Chapter 8

7. "Numbers 25," *Jamieson-Fausset-Brown Bible Commentary, Bible Hub*, https://biblehub.com/commentaries/jfb/numbers/25.htm.

8. "Numbers 25:4," *Bible Hub,* https://biblehub.com/numbers/25-4.htm.

8. "Commentaries: Numbers 25:4," *Bible Hub*, https://biblehub.com/commentaries/numbers/25-4.htm.

Chapter 9

5. Slick, Matt, "Why were only the virgins left alive among the Midianites in Numbers 31:17-18?", *Christian Apologetics and Research Ministry,* November 28, 2008, https://carm.org/bible-difficulties/why-were-only-the-virgins-left-alive-among-the-midianites-in-numbers-3117-18.

5. "Why did God command the Israelites to completely destroy the Midianites in Numbers 31:17?", *Got Questions Ministries*, accessed February 21, 2023, https://www.gotquestions.org/Numbers-31-17-Midianites.html.

Chapter 10

Thoughts to Ponder, Question 3: "How was God Himself the inheritance of the Levites?", *Got Questions Ministries*, accessed February 21, 2023, https://www.gotquestions.org/God-inheritance-Levites.html.

[Sidebar] "Levitical Cities," *Encyclopedia of the Bible*, Bible Gateway, https://www.biblegateway.com/resources/encyclopedia-of-the-bible/Levitical-Cities.

Also by Marilynn E. Hood

Daniel: Esteemed by God
Finding Peace in a Changing World

Does God care when things go wrong in our lives? Daniel and his friends must have asked themselves that question as they faced captivity, unfair politics, and even death sentences. Time after time, Daniel asked God for help—for hope—and God answered! Although the accounts in Daniel may seem far removed from the reality of life today, the truth is that the God who guided and protected His people back then is the same God who cares for you today.

The powerful stories and prophecies in the book of Daniel are exciting and, at times, confusing. In truth, not even Daniel himself understood everything he wrote about. But here's the good news: He didn't have to understand everything to have a close relationship with God; he simply needed to believe God and trust Him.

Daniel: Esteemed by God reveals the beautiful message of God's faithful love and continual presence in our lives. What Daniel and his friends discovered remains true in today's constantly changing world: God is in control. By relying on Him, you can find peace, even in the direst of circumstances.

Designed to be accessible for Bible students and novices alike, this book—with its short chapters, complete scripture references, and thought-provoking questions—makes this Old Testament book personally relevant. Most importantly, *Daniel: Esteemed by God* will help you better understand how to have a close relationship with God and experience His love in a deeper way.

"Daniel: Esteemed by God is a welcome and refreshing guide to understanding more of the tiny divine insights we are privileged to experience, if we have our spiritual eyes, ears, and minds attuned for the reception."
—**Dan Miller**, author of *Wisdom Meets Passion*

"Marilynn Hood masterfully shows the hand of God at work in Daniel and how that same hand is at work for us.... *Daniel: Esteemed by God* is a book for our times."
—**Debbie W. Wilson**, author of *Little Women, Big God*

MarilynnHood.com/daniel
info@courageousheartpress.com

Moses: Called By God

Living by Faith Through the Journeys of Life

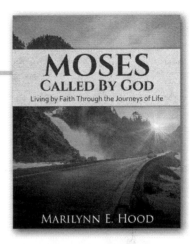

God's call on your life may seem impossible.

And maybe you've thought . . .

I'm not the one for the job.
I don't know how to do what You're asking me to do.
It's simply too much.
I'm exhausted by my responsibilities.

You aren't alone. When God called Moses to lead His people out of slavery, Moses begged God to choose someone else. Who could blame him? The job God had given Moses was massive! It seemed impossible. But God never expected Moses to do it alone.

Called by God to an extraordinary, life-changing journey, Moses led a fledgling nation of doubtful and often discontented people to the Promised Land. Along the way, he faced incredible challenges and disappointments. Moses also discovered a truth that remains today: God offers incomparable love and mercy to those who follow Him.

This study of Moses's life focuses on the relationship he had with God, a relationship he did not ask for or expect. Moses learned to trust God's goodness and faithfulness, and he experienced the kind of closeness that God desires to have with you today.

"Moses's story offers a gentle reminder to be listening for those burning bush moments when God can clarify our purpose and calling."

—**Dan Miller**, *New York Times* bestselling author of *48 Days to the Work You Love*, and host of the *48 Days Podcast*

"The insights and questions Marilynn offers help us understand that, like Moses, we can experience a deep and extraordinary relationship with God, which is exactly what He created us for!"

—**Meredith Perryman**, speaker, Bible teacher, and author of *The Whole Story*

"If you're wondering if God has called you or what His purpose is for you, this reflective study will help you find the answers."

—**Bill Rieser**, pastor, author, evangelist, and founder of Encounter Ministries

"Bible students and teachers alike will find lots of helpful information and inspiration in *Moses: Called by God.*"

—**Debbie W. Wilson**, author of *Little Strength, Big God*

MarilynnHood.com/moses
info@courageousheartpress.com

About The Author

Marilynn E. Hood is a Christian who has studied the Bible for most of her life. She draws upon her own personal learning journey and years of teaching experience in presenting these lessons.

Marilynn holds an MBA from Texas A&M University, where she later joined the faculty in the Department of Finance and taught the principles of personal finance to thousands of students. She also taught the principles of insurance in the CERTIFIED FINANCIAL PLANNER™ Program offered by Texas A&M University's Department of Agricultural Economics.

Marilynn is the author of *Daniel: Esteemed by God, Moses: Called by God*, and a personal finance book, *Money for Life*. Having retired from university teaching, she and her husband of fifty-three years, David Hood, currently reside on their farm near Bryan, Texas. They are the parents of three children and, more importantly, the grandparents to seven wonderful grandchildren and one adorable great-granddaughter.

MarilynnHood.com
Facebook.com/MarilynnHoodAuthor

Made in the USA
Columbia, SC
11 September 2024

41626769R00062